April [illegible]

To Yola

Dear friend for more than
fifty-five years
With love and admiration

Gary

Making a Life in Yorkville

Recent Titles in
Contributions in Sociology

Making a Life in Yorkville

*Experience and Meaning in the
Life-Course Narrative of an Urban
Working-Class Man*

Gerald Handel

Contributions in Sociology, Number 130

Greenwood Press
Westport, Connecticut • London

Library of Congress Cataloging-in-Publication Data

Handel, Gerald.
  Making a life in Yorkville : experience and meaning in the life-course narrative of an urban working-class man / by Gerald Handel.
      p.   cm.—(Contributions in sociology, ISSN 0084–9278 ; no. 130)
  Includes bibliographical references and index.
  ISBN 0–313–31307–5 (alk. paper)
  1. Middle-aged men—New York (State)—New York.   2. Working class—New York (State)—New York.   3. City and town life—New York (State)—New York.   4. Yorkville (New York, N.Y.)—Social conditions.   5. Yorkville (New York, N.Y.)—Economic conditions.   I. Title.   II. Series.
HQ1090.5.N7 H35   2000
305.38′9623′09747—dc21   99–049048

British Library Cataloguing in Publication Data is available.

Library of Congress Catalog Card Number: 99–049048
ISBN: 0–313–31307–5
ISSN: 0084–9278

First published in 2000

Greenwood Press, 88 Post Road West, Westport, CT 06881
An imprint of Greenwood Publishing Group, Inc.
www.greenwood.com

Printed in the United States of America

The paper used in this book complies with the Permanent Paper Standard issued by the National Information Standards Organization (Z39.48–1984).

10 9 8 7 6 5 4 3 2 1

To the memory of
Fred Davis

and to the memory of
Harry M. Rosen

and to
Yola Lev
Ira O. Glick
Carol and Lee Rainwater

Their talents for friendship have warmed my life.

Usual social-science concepts of the life cycle focus upon the flow of persons through time. But a mature human consciousness is also a compound resultant of the flow of time through persons.

David W. Plath (1980, p.13)

It is important that the standardized life course as we discuss it is an institutional system, a set of rules and preferences of a formalized but highly abstract kind. There is a great deal of slippage when it becomes translated into the actual experience of individuals, whose real life courses have more anomalies and unpredictabilities than the official system.

John W. Meyer (1986, p. 203)

Rather than looking at social and cultural systems solely as they impinge on a life, shape it, and turn it into an object, a life history should allow one to see how an actor makes culturally meaningful history, how history is produced in action and in the actor's retrospective reflections on that action. A life history narrative should allow one to see the subjective mapping of experience, the working out of a culture and a social system that is often obscured in a typified account.

Ruth Behar (1990, p. 225)

Contents

Preface

This study of the life of a working-class man is intended as a contribution to understanding how human lives proceed. It falls within a domain known by the overlapping terms "life course" and "human development." It uses a method known as "life history." It offers some new concepts in its domain and a new procedure for employing the method. The audience to which it is addressed includes scholars and students in all fields that are concerned with the life course and life-span development: sociology, psychology, human development, anthropology, social work, oral history, education, gerontology, counseling; it is also addressed to those who have a particular interest in the methodology of life history, narrative, and case study.

This study also throws new light on what kinds of events and experiences enter into a life lived in the urban working class. The life history of Tony Santangelo, a 47-year-old construction worker, offers, I believe, one of the fullest and most rounded accounts of a working-class man's life to be found in the literature. Inasmuch as Yorkville, one of New York's most historic neighborhoods in the Borough of Manhattan, is gradually disappearing as it becomes part of the gentrified Upper East Side, this study of one of its residents also makes a modest contribution to urban history, since it portrays the neighborhood and a community's way of life through his eyes.

The study of the life course through the study of a life history is not an entirely novel approach but it is not very widely used. Life-course studies more commonly are conducted with large data sets, so it is necessary to make clear what the approach taken here can contribute that is not attainable through large data sets. The present study is distinctive in these respects:

(1) It amplifies the concept of life course. As ordinarily studied, the life course is defined as a sequence of life transitions that have an essentially public character, transitions such as leaving school, getting a first job, getting married. Such events are, of course, also included in life histories, but many different aspects of a life—non-public events, self evaluations, dilem-

mas, moral judgments, triumphs and defeats—are included as well. What this volume offers is an account of a man's life course as he has experienced it and is able to tell of his experience. Whereas conventional studies most often deal with *the expectable life course*, this one deals with *the experienced life course*.

(2) Whereas studies of the expectable life course focus on factors that influence the timing and duration of statuses, this study is focused on how meanings are constructed in a person's life. It views the life course not as prescribed pathway or as statistical probability but as a personally and interpersonally constructed array of meanings within a social world that offers choice as well as imposing constraint.

(3) It offers the distinctive advantages of a case study, a methodology whose current value is signalled by several recent books devoted to it. Social scientists who regard generalization as the only goal of research challenge case study with the question: "How can you generalize from a single case?" By restrictively defining knowledge as valid generalization of empirical findings, those who ask this question as a dismissal of case study choose to avoid reciprocal questions: "What kinds of knowledge are lost in the establishment of generalizations? What important things can we learn that cannot be learned through the procedures that must be followed for arriving at empirical generalizations but are knowable through other procedures?" Knowledge grows by specification as well as by generalization. What a case study shows us that cannot be shown in large data sets are the specifics of action, the construction of reality through interpretation and communication. In large data sets, lives are aggregated; such an aggregation is, for some purposes, a meaningful unit, but it is not the only meaningful unit. An individual life is also a meaningful unit, as the large extant literatures of biography, autobiography, and life history attest.

(4) Finally, a case study permits a certain kind of generalization—not empirical generalization to other cases but the genesis of meaningful concepts, theories, and questions that have general applicability beyond the case. By close scrutiny of a case and its workings we can be prompted to think of questions that are significant for a range of cases and to produce concepts that can be useful for general understanding beyond the case that prompted their creation. That is what I have tried to do here. I offer a new way of thinking about the life course and a number of new concepts, as well as a more systematic use of some existing concepts than has been customary. Some years ago a younger colleague who, like I, was gathering some life histories because of their tantalizing promise of illumination, asked me "What do you do with life histories?" I did not then have a good answer, but I believe that I have, in this work, now provided a good answer, one that I hope others will find useful. Needless to say, no answer is ever the only answer. Just as my reading of and thinking about the work of others has led

me to see openings to new concepts and procedural improvements, I hope that readers of this work will be able to derive similar benefits.

This study is in three parts, preceded by a prologue that states my general orientation to the life course. Part I sets the conceptual and contextual framework of the study. Part II, after a brief introduction, consists of the verbatim, unedited life history recounted to the author by Tony Santangelo. Since the interviewee was promised anonymity, the name is a pseudonym, as are the names of family members and other key persons in his life. No other details of the recounted life history have been changed in any way.

Part III is my analysis of Tony Santangelo's life history. It seeks to understand the important aspects of his life that he has recounted. A great many life histories are being gathered these days by social scientists and historians. Many of them are not interpreted at all but are presented as documents simply demonstrating or exemplifying a social condition. Some do receive interpretation, primarily as exemplars of a culture. A few receive the kind of analysis offered here: that is, an analysis that conceives of the person not simply as an exemplar of a culture or of a social condition but as a person making choices within a social and cultural domain, a person faced with the task of having to construct a life within a society whose guidelines are sometimes insistent but often suggestive rather than precisely prescriptive and flexible rather than rigid. The analysis has the double aim of understanding one man's life and providing a new conceptualization and procedure for understanding other lives as well.

Just as a life is part of a community and society, so, too, is an analysis part of a community of discourse. Although this work is innovative in several respects, it is not idiosyncratic but enters into dialogue with historical and contemporary works bearing on issues of life course, life-span development, narrative, life history, self, social class, and gender. While it is not my purpose to present extended discussions of these literatures or of all the issues they raise, the contextual analysis of Part I, the Introduction to Part II, and the analysis of Tony Santangelo's life course in Part III each engage with significant statements from those literatures. These selections serve both as links to the discourse community and as benchmarks for the analysis. But they are *selections*, which help to place the analysis in a larger context. They are not, and are not intended to be, extended discussions of the issues embedded in the larger literatures.

NOTE

Because this is a book about a man, for stylistic consistency I use masculine nouns and pronouns in general statements, although most of them would be equally applicable to women.

Acknowledgments

My first debt for this volume is to Charles I. Katze, formerly Executive Director of the Stanley Isaacs Neighborhood Center in Yorkville, who generously supported my effort to gather life histories from working-class men and introduced me to Tony Santangelo. I was the beneficiary of Tony's trust in and respect for Chuck. Tony agreed to be interviewed, as did several other men, because Chuck vouched for me. I am grateful for his support, which also included providing me a private room in the Center for the interviews.

I am indebted to Tony Santangelo (pseudonym) for agreeing to share his life history with me and to answer my questions. He was comfortable in the interview situation, as was I. We were on a first-name basis. My sense is that he enjoyed his participation, and when I presented him with a copy of the transcript in a hard-cover binder he communicated pleasant surprise at the volume of his accomplishment.

The tape-recorded interviews were transcribed by the Oral History Research Office of Columbia University. I express my appreciation to Mrs. Elizabeth Mason, formerly Associate Director of that office, for agreeing to take responsibility for the transcription and selecting one of her transcribers to do the work. That transcript forms the bulk of Part II of this volume. One colleague who read the transcript commented to me that it seems more fluent than the transcripts he has seen in the work of that group of sociologists known as conversation analysts; he thought I had edited it to increase the fluency. I have not edited it in any way except to provide pseudonyms for actual names; to delete a few words that the transcriber had crossed out and replaced with what s/he considered more accurate renditions (which were usually slight variants on the crossed-out words); to provide a blank line in place of two or three uniquely identifying facts about persons other than Tony; and to insert "(inaudible)" in the two or three blank spaces where a word is missing. In my judgment, these measures have no significance philosophically, methodologically, or theoretically, except that they protect the privacy of Tony and others whom he mentions. In all other respects, the transcript is identical to that produced by the transcriber. While Tony was fairly articulate, his narration was also characterized by grammatical errors, hesitancies and self-interruptions, and some syntactical awkwardness. These have all been retained in the text. The text before the reader is the same text that I worked with, unaltered in wording or sequence.

Several friends and colleagues offered particularly helpful comments on the manuscript and substantial encouragement at critical junctures. For this support I thank Spencer Cahill, Ronald Farrell, Viktor Gecas, Norman Goodman, Joseph Gusfield, Barbara Levy Simon, and Kate Wittenberg. It was Barbara Levy Simon's suggestion that I introduce the life course narrative in Part II with some pointed questions, rather than simply having Part II consist only of the narrative, as I originally intended. Although I was initially skeptical, when I set to work formulating the questions I realized that her suggestion was most valuable. I want also to express my thanks to Richard Alba, Robert Alford, and Lindsey Churchill for their generosity in taking the time to read the manuscript and offering me their views. Although their views differ from mine in important ways, their comments were helpful.

My wife, Ruth, far more skilled than I in computer use, has given me much guidance and assistance in dealing with its mysteries. I am most appreciative of her substantial help and steadfast moral support.

I thank Ellen Smiley, director of the Center for Teaching and Learning at CCNY for making available the Center's scanner and the services of her staff members, Bill Jeanniton and Jason Von Zerneck. I worked most closely with Bill, who was enormously helpful in assisting me to scan the life history interviews into the computer, and Jason was promptly and generously helpful when Bill was not available. They have my respect and my thanks.

I want to express my great appreciation to Elisabetta Linton, who, as Acquisitions Editor for Greenwood Publishing Group, recognized the merits of this work. I also thank her successor, Suzanne Staszak-Silva, for continuing support. Thanks also to all at Greenwood who helped produce and market this book.

Financial support for my work with life histories was provided by the Small Grants Branch of the National Institute of Mental Health; a small grant from The City College; and a grant from the Institute on Pluralism and Group Identity, through the generosity of its Director, Irving M. Levine.

Prologue: Making a Life

Every man depends upon his society for a meaningful life, any kind of life. Every child is born somewhere, a socially defined place, and every child who survives is born into the care of someone. Every child is born into some memberships—into a family or foster care, a community, a nation, perhaps into a religion, an ethnic group, a grouping of kin, a network of relationships which operate in established ways. And so a child starts out in life unable to function in society, yet located in it by the fact that the groupings into which he is born have their place. Their place is his place, their rules the rules he must learn, and their routines the ones he must acquire. In the course of his life he moves on to other groupings in other settings. In their midst—earlier and later—he finds the tasks that will occupy him, the interests that will engage him, the standards by which he will judge himself and others. As a person moves through his life course, his sense of who he is and what he is about takes shape in relation to others whose lives and activities are organized into groups and institutions that serve to focus purposes, emotions, activities, and plans—from day to day, month to month, year to year. He becomes closely involved in some groups and institutions, peripherally involved in others, and aware of still others from a distance. Throughout his life, a person finds membership and seeks satisfying involvement with different kinds of groups and institutions—family, friendships, work groups, recreation groups, impersonal associations organized for various purposes.

Every man's life is subject to probabilities that certain kinds of experiences and outcomes are more likely than others, but men sometimes perceive and struggle with the probabilities bearing in on them, and they reach for a different fate. A man's life chances are influenced by the station to which he is born, but people are not simply passive exemplars of their birth station. Further,in a large-scale urban society, culture is not a script but a range of variously valued options and an array of expectations of different degrees of demandingness. A particular subculture may have many or few prescriptions and proscriptions, but these do not construct themselves into actions. Their relevance to a situation must be interpreted by a human agent. Every person develops consciousness and must come to his own changing understanding of the constraints that limit him, the social supports that may sustain him, the possibilities open to him, the choices that he can make. Whatever the combination of skill and blunder with which he makes his way, he cannot be totally inert or oblivious in his circumstance, even if he does not always understand it. The world is defined and redefined for him by multiple significant others who look at the world from their own incompletely overlapping understandings and who exert their uneven influences upon him. He must make his own adaptations to situations that are visited upon him or to situations he selects to enter. Every man must make his own life.

Every man must remember his life in order to continue living as the person he believes himself to be. No one can remember all that he has lived through. It is, indeed, necessary to forget much, but to forget all is to lose the capacity to continue social participation except as an institutionalized patient or equivalent. The social scientist can deal with memory in terms of its limitations or in terms of its necessity as a foundation of personal and social existence. The limitations of memory may lead some researchers to try to avoid any reliance upon the memories of those they study. What we remember is indeed incomplete, influenced by "an interplay of appetites, instincts, interests and ideals peculiar to any given subject," as Bartlett (1932) pointed out long ago, and subject to repression, as Freud (1948 [1915]) pointed out even earlier. Yet, we also confront the phenomenon that people not only must remember a great deal about their lives in order to function but that they have the capacity to assemble their memories in a recounting that they recognize and claim as the story of their life. There are undoubtedly contexts in which life history recounters deliberately lie, but there are also contexts in which recounters strive earnestly for veridicality. Although we need to be attentive to the vagaries of memory, we ought also to heed a conclusion by Daniel Schacter, one of the leading contemporary researchers of memory who states that "we must keep in mind that errors and distortions in remembering, though startling when they occur, are far from the norm in our mnemonic lives. Most of the time our memories reliably handle the staggering variety of demands that our day-to-day activities place on them" (Schacter 1996, pp. 132–133). Long-term memory adds complications, but let us not forget that the capacity to remember and tell one's life history forms the basis of the art of autobiography and has been the foundation of the life history method in social science since the work of Thomas and Znaniecki (1918–1920). Remembering and telling one's life history is a fundamental human accomplishment.

PART I

The Multiple Contexts of an Experienced Life Course

THE LIFE

THE COMMUNITY CONTEXT

Yorkville, now slowly dissolving into the gentrifying Upper East Side of Manhattan, was long known as one of New York City's more distinctive neighborhoods, occasionally reaching into public consciousness almost as vividly as Harlem, Greenwich Village, and the Lower East Side. It was known for its multi-ethnic population of European descent—Germans, Irish, Czechs, Italians, Hungarians, Austrians—all of whom maintained a variety of cultural institutions and commercial establishments. It gained brief national notoriety during the 1930s when the German-American Bund, a pro-Nazi organization, conducted parades through the neighborhood in support of Germany's dictator, Adolf Hitler, and his totalitarian state, the Third Reich—parades that generated tumultuous counterdemonstrations. More benign, Yorkville was the birthplace of Lou Gehrig, legendary first baseman of the New York Yankees in their glory days, as well as the locale of the Ruppert Brewery whose owner, Jacob Ruppert, was then also the owner of the Yankees.

The population of the district was largely working-class, some very poor, although streets on the perimeter of the neighborhood housed more well-to-do people. Housing for a large share of the population was cold-water flats in four- and five-story tenements. Many of the tenements, still occupied by working-class people, remain, particularly on the side streets. But along the avenues many have been torn down and replaced by high-rise apartment buildings for young upwardly mobile professionals—"yuppies" as they came to be known in the 1980s. If stories in *The New York Times* are any indication, Yorkville's fading color is newsworthy. Over a double-column story with two pictures, a headline of December 21, 1980 reads, "Change Comes as a Loss to Yorkville Old-Timers" (*New York Times*

1980). The story records the closing of Joe Wagner's, a restaurant and bar that was a favorite working-class meeting place—and was frequented by Tony Santangelo and his friends. One of the pictures shows the owner, his wife, and a cook. The other shows a new 29-story high-rise towering over a 5-story tenement next to it. A 1984 headline reports "The Fall of a Yorkville Landmark: Ethnic Makes Way for Modern" (Kennedy 1984), while one of 1991 records "Durable Landmark to Irish Glory Fading Out on the East Side" (*New York Times* 1991). These and other specific stories over recent years can be partially summed up by the headline of November 6, 1983: "Yorkville Turns Chic and Costly" (Rimer 1983). The newspaper continued to chronicle the transformation in occasional stories over the years. One 1985 story quotes a 45-year resident, a retired foodservice worker, now age 75, who lives with his wife on Social Security payments of $400 a month, while adjacent paragraphs refer to studio and one-bedroom apartments in renovated buildings renting for $1,000 a month and one-bedroom condominiums selling for $200,000 in new buildings (Johnson 1985). In 1990 a story about new condominiums and "upscale shops" was headlined "A New Cachet for Old East 86th Street" (Kennedy 1990).

Tony Santangelo's Yorkville

What was it like to grow up in Yorkville? How did Tony Santangelo experience its distinctiveness? Born and bred in Yorkville, having spent most of his life there, and still living there in 1974 when he told his life history at the age of 47, Tony had a firm identity as a Yorkville resident. What did Yorkville mean to him?

In telling his life story, Tony Santangelo reveals the local social structure as he participated in it. He identifies himself as a child of Italian-American parents. However, as he recounts his life, his ethnic identity did not loom large in his social participation. Far more central was being Catholic and the stability of his membership in the same parish. His christening, communion, and confirmation all took place at Our Lady of Good Counsel parish church, in which his parents had been married. Tony went to the parish elementary school and graduated from it. (He went to a public high school.) He was married in that church and his children were christened in it. In his late teens and early twenties he played baseball on the team of neighboring St. Ignatius parish, whose membership was much wealthier than his native parish and included some of the celebrity Catholic families of New York and the nation. Through this athletic participation out of his local neighborhood he gained an awareness of social class differences. Because of his ability as a player, he was invited to delimited participation in a world of privilege. He speaks with wonder and even awe as he recollects the St. Ignatius team's being provided with top-quality equipment and, for the first time in his life, playing baseball in a proper baseball uniform. While he did not long sustain off-the-field friendships with his St. Ignatius teammates, he was part of a successful team, one that did well enough in its Catholic Youth Organization league to travel to the CYO national championships in Michigan. This was an early highlight in his life, even though the team suffered losses in its first two games and quickly returned to New York.

Tony never gives any inkling of ever hoping to become rich and move into an adult world like that of St. Ignatius parish. But he is unambiguous and emphatic in his determination to avoid sinking from his poor working-class status to what he regards as the bottom of society, the status of criminal law-breaker. He talks about the guys in his neighborhood who engaged in crime and who tried to get him to join in with them. Although he acknowledges pilfering apples and potatoes from grocers, he makes a clear distinction between that and more serious crime; he also makes it clear that he never stepped over what he sees as a clear dividing line. Indeed, he delineates the choice he saw between being involved in crime or being involved in sports, and he determined to follow his love of baseball, which gave him not only intrinsic rewards but an effective way to stay out of trouble. Sports became an important anchorage for his life, not only in adolescence and young adulthood but in adulthood, when he was asked by a priest he was friendly with to coach baseball and hockey teams in the parish. The priest's request effected a transformation of Tony's identity, because not until then did Tony think of himself as someone who had something to teach. Tony's involvement with baseball dramatizes what may be taken as *twin principles of the life course: Every life is a social construction, and every life is a personal construction. Neither principle is reducible to the other, and neither is sufficient by itself.* Tony's family and his parish gave him membership in the social world. These social units delineated behavior standards, held out goals and opportunities, offered guidance toward respected and worthwhile activity. The life of the neighborhood and the street also offered choices, and Tony is explicit about choices that he made.

Parishes were thus significant units of social meaning in Tony's life. St. Ignatius parish was both his introductory instruction about a world of wealth beyond what he knew in his home parish and his personal anchorage as an athlete whose accomplishments were recognized beyond his immediate circle. One of the most poignant expressions in Tony's account of his life is his statement, "I always wanted to be somebody, but I just became, just like a neighborhood somebody." He was good enough to receive tryouts with three major league baseball teams, but none materialized into a chance at a career.

THE HISTORICAL CONTEXT

Every person's life occurs in historical time and is shaped by the events, social structure, and culture of that time, even as the person engages with immediate others in constructing that life. Tony Santangelo was born in 1927, during the post-World War I "normalcy" of the 1920s, as proclaimed by President Harding and continued by his Republican successors, presidents Coolidge and Hoover. His childhood years were mostly lived during the Great Depression that began in 1929 and that continued even during the emergency relief and social welfare reform efforts of President Franklin D. Roosevelt's New Deal, until the country's economic situation changed around 1940 when production increased in anticipation of possible war. His adolescence was passed during World War II. When the war ended in 1945 he entered the army and participated in the occupation of Japan. Three years after he completed his army service, the Korean War broke out and lasted for three years. When Tony was interviewed, the Vietnam War had concluded a year or so earlier. In addition to these several wars and the Great Depression, other historically significant periods during his life were "the McCarthy era," the several years in the early 1950s when Senator Joseph R. McCarthy of Wisconsin conducted relentless and out-of-control searches for Communist subversives; the "Great Society" (1963–1968) of President Lyndon Johnson, which overlapped the Vietnam War; and a long period of political instability beginning with the assassination of President John Kennedy in November 1963 and followed by the open turmoil of the Civil Rights movement, the protests against the Vietnam War, the assassinations of civil rights leader Dr. Martin Luther King and presidential candidate Senator Robert F. Kennedy, and the political scandal known as "Watergate," which resulted in the resignation of President Richard Nixon in 1974, a few months after Tony was interviewed.

Since a major part of Tony Santangelo's formation of consciousness took place during the Great Depression, it is a plausible supposition that the economic deprivations and hardships sustained by so many people during that time would have had a significant impact on his life. We are cautioned against applying it uncritically by Glen Elder's study (1974) of children of this period, which found that the impact of the Great Depression depended on the age of the child when it hit and on how much economic hardship the child's family suffered. Tony reports that his family always had enough to eat. His father seems to have been steadily employed as a bartender in his brother's restaurant, and Tony recalls with some vividness the way in which his father practiced his occupation. But Tony also refers to a sense of not enough money available, which he attributes to his father's spending on drink, not to the Depression. His most acute expression of economic deprivation comes in his exclamation that he did not live in an apartment with steam heat until 1959. He communicates a sense of humiliation that his housing was in this respect so far below a contemporary standard. This was a prevalent tenement condition that pre-existed the Depression and continued for him long after it but that does not appear to have been in any way a direct consequence of it.

Of all the defining political and economic events of his lifetime until age forty-seven, the only two that Tony Santangelo treats as personally significant are the United States participation in World War II and the United States Army's occupation of Japan after the Japanese defeat in that war. His older brother was drafted into the army when Tony was thirteen and was still overseas when Tony went into the army at age eighteen in 1945. His brother's absence during those five teenage years did not diminish Tony's idolization of his brother, but it did deprive him of the day-to-day living example that his brother might have provided. The possible significance of that deprivation can be judged by considering Tony's characterization of his brother in the context of his own life course. The occupation of Japan was a political event in which he personally participated. It is the only substantial period of his life when he was away from Yorkville, and he sees it as having enlarged his life.

The historical context of a life is constructed not only of political and economic events and trends but of cultural ones as well. The creation of the movies expanded the opportunities for children, as well as adults, to "go out," as historian David Nasaw has documented in his book, *Going Out* (Nasaw 1994). In Tony's case movie going played a significant part in constructing his relationship with his mother. Baseball, in those days celebrated as "the national pastime," was another significant cultural focus; it provided Tony with his early aspiration, with meaning in his father's eyes, and with an important adult identity. Finally, at mid-life when he produced his life history, attachment to urban neighborhood was still a value, although it was being eroded by real estate forces that were slowly encroaching on a long-settled neighborhood. Although as a young man he moved for a brief period to the Bronx, he soon moved back to Yorkville and was living at mid-life in the same urban neighborhood in which he was born and had grown up.

Every life course is a product of its time in history, but it cannot be understood only in historical terms. The limits of an historical approach are acknowledged by Glen Elder, who, with the publication of his 1974 study of Depression-era children, became one of the leading scholars of historical influence on the life course. In a methodological work devoted to working with archival data, Elder, Eliza Pavalko, and Elizabeth S. Clipp (1993, p. 67) state, "[E]ven when historical influence is substantively important it may be operationalized as a period or cohort effect that provides no precise information as to the nature of the influence. We know that members of a particular cohort are not uniformly exposed to the historical record and that experiential variations within specific cohorts are substantial." It is therefore necessary, as I believe this statement implies, to focus on ways of gaining access to and understanding the experienced life course, which is the goal of the present work. The next two sections take us some steps closer to that goal, while Parts II and III present its attainment.

THE LIFE HISTORY

THE NARRATIVE CONTEXT

Every life history is a social product because it is produced in a language that belongs to a society and because it is produced for an audience (even if the audience is restricted to the socialized person who produced it). But the circumstances in which life histories are produced are quite various, and the variations are of several kinds. Denzin (1989) reviews the variety of ways in which lives are told and subsumes them all into a general concept of method which he calls "the interpretive biographical method." He makes various distinctions within it, but I want to emphasize one distinction more sharply than he does.

A fundamental distinction that is important for present purposes is between a life history that is written over a long period of time by a person who initiates the project of telling his own life and a life history that is produced in interviews in response to someone else's initiative. These two procedures arise from different traditions, and they yield two different kinds of products that—despite some occasional blurring of terminology—go by different names. The written document is regularly referred to as an autobiography, and it is a crafted product written to produce certain impressions or effects that can be carefully controlled by the writer. Writers of autobiographies are usually prominent persons whose eminent (or notorious) social standing establishes a claim on public attention.[1] That claim is not restricted to the documentary dimension of autobiography. As Georges Gusdorf writes:

> The significance of autobiography should . . . be sought beyond truth and falsity, as those are conceived by simple common sense. It is unquestionably a document about a life, and the historian has a perfect right to check out its testimony and verify its accuracy. But it is also a work of art, and the literary devotee, for his part, will be aware of its stylistic harmony and the beauty of its images. (Gusdorf 1980, p. 43)

In contrast, many, if not most, scholars who obtain life histories through an interviewing procedure are not primarily interested in them as art but for what they reveal about the life and how it is lived. The cooperative recounter of a life history is less likely to be intent on constructing a focused and unified picture of his life and certainly less likely to be able to do so on the spot. Although impression management may be a constitutive element in every social interaction, a life history produced in response to interviewer questions that are not known in advance is likely to yield a less carefully controlled product. The ultimate evaluation of the life history in this respect can be arrived at by considering the context in which the life history was obtained, as well as by indicators of the recounter's readiness to be forthcoming and to strive for veridicality. The reader of Tony Santangelo's life history is likely to judge that he is ingenuous and forthright.

Tony Santangelo was the second of a dozen Yorkville men whose life histories I obtained. I had originally attempted to obtain interviewees by writing letters on City College stationery explaining my purpose to men living in the Stanley Isaacs Houses and Holmes Towers, two New York City public housing projects in Yorkville. My follow-up phone calls resulted only in refusals. I received help in gaining referrals from Charles I. Katze, then Executive Director of the Stanley Isaacs Neighborhood Center, adjacent to the projects. He acted as intermediary and introduced me to my first few life history informants, some of whom lived in the projects and some in the tenements on the nearby streets. Tony had been a tenement dweller but had moved into the projects eight years before. I told Katze that I wanted to obtain life histories from working-class men who had grown up in and lived most of their lives in Yorkville. I told him also that I would pay the men $4 per hour for their time.[2] He conveyed this information to Tony and to others who agreed to be interviewed. These initial life history informants subsequently helped recruit friends and acquaintances in a "snowball sample." Katze provided me with a room in the Stanley Isaacs Neighborhood Center where I could interview the men in privacy. They thus were interviewed in a building in their own neighborhood, one that was familiar and congenial. The interviews were tape recorded, and they were transcribed by the Oral History Research Office of Columbia University, which sought and retained a copy of the transcripts for its own archive. To each interviewee I gave a copy of his transcript in a hardcover binder.

Life histories are collected for many purposes. Anthropologists have long collected them as a means to illuminate the cultures of the life history informants (Kluckhohn 1945; Langness 1965; Langness and Frank 1981; Watson and Watson-Franke 1985). Sociologists have solicited written autobiographies to illuminate delinquency (Shaw 1966 [1930]; Bennett 1981), as well as life history interviews to explain entry into an occupation (Berteaux and Berteaux 1981). Psychologists have collected them to study personality development (Allport 1942; Frenkel 1936; White 1952; McAdams 1988). Feminist scholars have gathered life histories to document the particular qualities of women's lives (Behar 1990, 1993; Patai 1988a, 1988b; Personal Narratives Group 1989).

One feature common to many (though not all) such efforts, regardless of the researcher's goal, was that the researcher sustained an acquaintance of long duration with the life history interviewee. The life history was obtained over a period of months or even years of research, and Plummer seems to maintain that that is the only correct procedure (Plummer 1983, p. 14; cf. also Langness 1965, p. 35.) Such extended interview time may be necessary or desirable in many research situations, but it should not be regarded as an inflexible rule of methodology. Adequate sponsorship may yield suitable access in a short time frame. The study presented here, as well as related studies in collateral papers (Handel 1984, 1991, 1994) undertakes to show that a considerable and significant understanding of the experienced life course can be gained from life histories that are obtained in a much shorter time and do not depend upon developing an extended relationship with the life history informants. The life history of Tony Santangelo was obtained in two interviews six days apart, the first lasting three hours and the second two hours. The resulting transcript of 145 double-spaced pages was one of the two briefest of the twelve men whom I interviewed. While there is little question that more interviewing time extended over a longer acquaintance would probably have yielded more information, that proposition begs the methodological question, which is: Can we learn sufficient information from a two- or three-interview life history to portray convincingly the experienced life course of the recounter, and can we gain from it sufficient understanding of underlying processes to justify additional efforts of this kind? This study was not conceived as an extended fieldwork study but as a specific type of qualitative interview study. Many researchers are likely to be similarly situated, able to commit five to ten hours to gathering a life history, but not months or years. While each reader will have to make his or her own judgment regarding the methodological question, my own conviction is that Tony Santangelo's life history is one of the fullest and most comprehensive recent portraits of an ordinary, urban working-class man in early middle age. In addition, I believe that the interpretive effort I have made in Part III presents concepts that improve our understanding of his experienced life course and offers guidelines that may be used for understanding the experienced life course of women as well as men, and adults of any age.

Thus far I have distinguished among three ways of producing a life history. The initial distinction is between an *autobiographer*, who writes the story of his life and produces a crafted account, and a *recounter*, who responds to interviewer initiative and questions, spontaneously drawing on his memory of his life. Within the latter category I made a further distinction between a life history gathered over an extended period of acquaintance with the subject and a life history gathered in two or three interviews conducted within one or two weeks and totaling between five and ten hours. No terminology exists for this distinction, so I propose to call them *acquaintance-based* and *interview-based* life histories. Although the former is also based on interview, the terms seem to me to convey a useful temporal and relational distinction.

The interview-based life history may seem to be vulnerable to thinness of information. Readers of Tony Santangelo's life history may wish that I had asked one or another further question not found in the transcription or that I had had one interview more to cover some areas not covered. (I also see places where I should have asked a follow-up question, and in Part III I discuss an important information gap that resulted.) The interview-based life history, as a way of finding out about lives, is at one end of a spectrum whose opposite pole is the longitudinal study. The longitudinal study, which gathers interviews and other information from subjects at successive times over a period of many years, even decades, would seem to be a more satisfactory way of finding out about lives. Yet, in addition to the fact that decades-long longitudinal studies are enormously expensive and therefore few in number, the belief that they are comprehensive in their informativeness by virtue of their decades-long data gathering may well be an illusion. The words of John Clausen in this regard are sobering. In 1960, Clausen became the Director of the Institute of Human Development at the University of California, Berkeley. In that capacity he also took over directorship of the Oakland Growth Study established by Herbert Stolz and Harold E. Jones in 1931–32. Eleven- and twelve-year-old children were "observed, questioned, measured, and tested on more than a hundred different occasions" over a period of six years until they graduated from high school. When Clausen took over, a major follow-up study was being completed as these people neared age forty. And yet with all these data gathered in childhood and in adulthood, Clausen writes in his foreword to a study based on them, Glen Elder's well-regarded *Children of the Great Depression*:

> Even in longitudinal research there are inevitably gaps in one's knowledge. One could not possibly monitor or review all of the salient experiences of a single individual, even if one knew how to ask all of the relevant questions. (Clausen, in Elder, 1974, p. xviii)

Clausen is, of course, correct in this. But he tries to transcend these limitations by proposing, in his next sentence, "Under such circumstances, the richer and more diverse the data collected by earlier investigators, the greater the likelihood that their successors will be able to address research questions not previously formulated" (p. xviii). While there is some validity to this judgment, it also points to an unattainable, ever receding goal, since successors are always likely to have questions that have not and could not have been anticipated by their predecessors.

Understanding a life is a task without limit. It can never be completed because we can never know all there is to know. Even when a life is over, there are always new questions. And there will always be gaps in one's information, not to speak of limitations of perspicacity. Nevertheless, it is a challenge that fascinates and beckons, and if we work with the information we have and ask significant questions, we can presume to move toward some understanding of a life and of lives as processes. Tony Santangelo told us a great deal about his life in five hours of interview, enough to make it possible to seek understanding of it and to ask questions and formulate concepts that will be useful in understanding other lives as well.

The heading of this section, "The Narrative Context," has a double refer-ent. The discussion thus far has been about the context in which the oral narrative was obtained. Its presentation as a printed text is a second narra-tive context. In a generally laudatory review of three anthropological life histories, obtained by what I have called the acquaintance-based proce-dure, Crapanzano (1984) is critical of Shostak's (1981) life history of a !Kung woman because "she does not include her own interventions in 'Nisa's text'" (Crapanzano 1984, p. 957). He also notes that all three are given little analysis by the anthropologists who obtained and presented them (Crapan-zano 1984, p. 958). The present work contrasts with these in both respects. My questions and comments are retained, so that the reader can judge in what ways they have shaped the text. The reader can utilize this verbatim text to think about additional or alternative questions, better-phrased ques-tions, and alternative procedures for the entire enterprise. In addition, I provide, in Part III, an analysis of Tony Santangelo's life history, and the reader can utilize the text to evaluate the analysis, since the text has not been edited or rearranged. The reader has the entire identical text that I had.

THE THEORETICAL CONTEXT

Life histories are gathered for many purposes. Diversity of purpose, as well as of technique, is discussed by Kluckhohn (1945), Angell (1945), Langness and Frank (1981), and Watson and Watson-Franke (1985). John Dollard (1935) proposed a set of criteria to be used in evaluating all life his-tories. Gordon Allport (1942) criticized this effort on the grounds that "Dol-lard's criteria will not bring social scientists to agree on the value of a document. . . . The point is that while Dollard formulates his own prefer-ences he does not succeed in establishing objective standards by which to command the consent of his readers to his evaluations" (p. 27). But, given the diverse purposes for which life histories are gathered, the larger point to be made is that any effort to establish universal criteria is very likely in-appropriate and misdirected. Allport, for example, distinguishes between comprehensive and topical autobiographies. A comprehensive autobiog-raphy "is one that deals with a relatively large number of lines of experi-ence, giving a picture of variety, roundness and interrelatedness in the life" (Allport 1942, p. 77). A topical autobiography is "short and specialized in content" (p. 76). How could comprehensive and topical autobiographies be judged by the same criteria?

Disregarding Allport's use of "autobiography" as a generic term for all kinds of life histories, however produced, his distinction between compre-hensive and topical is a useful one. For example, the best known life history produced soon after Thomas and Znaniecki's (1918–1920) work is a topical one, Shaw's *The Jack-Roller, A Delinquent Boy's Own Story* (Shaw [1930] 1966), which focused on a boy's truancies, delinquencies, and arrests in an effort to understand how his delinquency developed into a delinquent career.[3] In contrast, my effort was to obtain a comprehensive life history from Tony Santangelo and the other men I interviewed. Whereas Shaw began by interviewing the boy to obtain an account of all his delinquencies and arrests, which were then arranged in a chronological sequence and returned to him in a list for use as a guide in writing his "own story" (Shaw 1966 [1930], p. 23), I began with a general instruction: "I'd like you to tell me the story of your life. Begin at the beginning and tell me as much as you remember. Then I'll ask you some questions." I specifically did not want to delineate any topics in advance. I defined the task as openly as I could because I wanted each man to construct his account as fully as possible in his own way. The fruitfulness of this open approach becomes quickly evident in the very different ways that they "begin at the beginning." (See the discussion of the difference between Tony Santangelo and Frank Schmidt in Handel 1994).

The openness of my approach corresponded to my purpose. I wanted to use life histories to open wider the study of the life course. At the outset I was not sure where my work would lead, but it was based on the general premise that human action is fundamentally interpretive. My general guide was W. I. Thomas's celebrated dictum: "If men define situations as real, they are real in their consequences." To be sure, I also had a general research issue in mind, the issue of continuity and discontinuity in the life course. Thus the question "How is childhood experience related to adult life?" was one that underlies this endeavor, and I return to it later in this section as well as in Part III. What I needed to work with were statements—life histories—that captured as pristinely as possible my informants' own construction of their lives.

As I worked on the project, it became clear to me that the term "the life course" is not a unitary construction. Initially, I had trouble relating what I was trying to do to the literature on the life course. I realized I had to address the difficulty by trying to clarify what it is about the life course that one learns from a life history and how that differs from what is learned about the life course from other kinds of data and procedures. While I do not attempt a comprehensive review of all the ways the term is used, I cite here a few leading uses and then state my own.

John Clausen (1986, p. 2) observes that "The life course is, by definition, a progression through time." He briefly examines several approaches that differ in their focus and in how they conceive of that progression. He defines his own goal as describing "the expectable life course" (p. 1), and this concept of expectability is implicit in other definitions. Elder and Rockwell (1979, pp. 2–3) state that "The life course refers to . . . social patterns in the timing, duration, spacing and order of events and roles . . . [T]he individual life course is comprised of interlocking careers, such as those of work, marriage, and parenthood."

More recently Elder and O'Rand (1995, p. 453) stated: "The life course represents a concept and a theoretical perspective. As a concept, it refers to age-graded life patterns embedded in social institutions and subject to historical change. The life course consists of interlocking trajectories or pathways across the life span that are marked by sequences of events and social transitions." Other scholars adopt similar conceptualizations. In seeking to draw a clear terminological distinction between "life span development" as used in psychology and "life course" as a sociological concept, Hagestad and Neugarten (1985, p. 35) state that "a life course approach concentrates on age-related transitions that are *socially created, socially recognized, and shared.*" Kohli (1986b, p. 271) argues that "the life course can be conceptualized as a social institution . . . a pattern of rules ordering a key dimension of life." Sørensen (1986, p. 178) writes that "because of the association between the positions an individual occupies and what this individual does, believes, and possesses, main features of individuals' life courses can be described by the major positions individuals occupy during their lifetime. Major positions are generally not occupied in a random order. It therefore becomes an important part of the sociology of the life course to describe and analyze the patterning of positions over the life span.

These brief quotations of several scholars' definitions of the life course cannot do justice either to the richness of their studies or to the full diversity of life course research. But, together, they do point to one very dominant trend in the field—looking at the life course as it is shaped by social structure. There is no escaping social structure; every life is shaped by it, but that is not all that goes into a life nor all that there is to be said about it.

The approaches entailed in the quoted definitions are valid approaches, but they leave out much. First, they leave out the perspective of the individual, for whom the social structure is not a well-charted path or a well-enclosed and well-marked series of corridors but a complex reality that is full of ambiguity, apprehended only gradually, understood incrementally and very imperfectly, and negotiated through trial and error. What is omitted from these approaches is a clear and decisive characterization of the human being as an interpretive being, who must interpret situations with a continuing mix of current perspective, retrospective recall, and prospective anticipated outcomes. Second, they don't pay much attention to what individuals feel about various aspects of their lives. They do not capture satisfaction, disappointment, and self-criticism nor elation, complacency, and dread. Third, by conceiving of the life course in terms of positions, events, rules, and careers, they leave out consideration of how people enjoy themselves, experiences of sociability, amusement and friendship. Fourth, they do not deal with flouting of rules as an experiential issue. In brief, social structural approaches to the life course are necessary but not sufficient.

The theoretical position underlying the study of the life course by the life history method can be stated in the following propositions, which develop and refine ideas first presented in Handel 1994: (1) A life history produces an account of a person's currently available biography. (2) It is made up of several kinds of constitutive elements—events, encounters, practices, emotions, relationships, interpretive judgments, and evaluations. (3) Through a sustained process of remembering and telling to the interviewer, the recounter constitutes his life course as an object which he claims as his own in the telling, which he claims as his life course as he has experienced it and knows it.[4] (4) Just as the self functions reflexively in all its transactions with social objects (Mead 1934), the production of a life history representing the experienced life course is a reflexive activity of the person's self. It is the product of an inner dialogue which arises in response to an interpersonal dialogue between interviewer and interviewee, and it becomes part of the latter. (5) The constitutive elements of the life history—including their syntax, sequence, and relative proportions—can be understood as having various kinds of symbolic meaning to the recounter. All represent various aspects of his life. They therefore provide a basis for additional analysis by an interpreter who wishes to utilize them for exploring the nature of and understanding the experienced life course as a domain of human experience.

The interpretive methodology in social science, long known by the Weberian keyword *verstehen* but now more commonly referred to as hermeneutic, is a generic concept that encompasses diverse approaches to interpretation. Two of these approaches, the Freudian psychoanalytic and the symbolic interactionist, have long been considered polar opposites. That opposition constituted for me the puzzle that led me to initiate an exploration of the life course through the life history method. A central point of contention is whether adult life should be interpreted as determined by earlier experience or whether it is essentially constructed and newly emergent in ongoing interaction. In the first third of the twentieth century, psychoanalytic theory developed by Freud viewed childhood experience as having a deterministic effect on later life. Philip Rieff summarized Freud's approach in these words:

> Freud took development for granted. That children become adults, that the lower becomes higher, the simple complex, the unknown known—such optimistic commonplaces he shunned. His desire was always to find, in emergence, sameness; in the dynamic, the static; in the present, latent pasts. (Rieff 1961, p. 237)

Freud's view exemplifies one of what Gergen (1980) has called the two established theories of the life course, "the stability account." The other he calls "the ordered change account." This type of theory, most prominently exemplified by Erikson (1950) and Levinson (1978), regards the person as passing through a series of predetermined stages. Despite their differences, both types of theory are deterministic. In Freud's version, childhood experience determines the forms of later experiences. In Erikson's and Levinson's versions, the life course consists of a series of built-in stages.

Gergen proposes a different alternative, which he calls "aleatoric." This type of theory "calls attention to the flexibility of developmental patterns. . . . From this perspective, existing patterns appear potentially evanescent, the unstable result of the particular juxtaposition of contemporary historical events" (1980, p. 34). The aleatoric perspective views the person "as an active agent, capable of self-direction and change" (Starr 1983).

The most absolute statement of this view is provided by Brim (1974) in an unpublished paper quoted by Starr: "any man can change in any way, at any time" (Starr 1983, p. 258.) How could this occur? It could occur because a person is capable of interpreting himself, his actions, his situation, his potentialities. Person as active interpreter is one of the core ideas of the symbolic interactionist theory of human behavior originating in the ideas of Charles Horton Cooley, W. I. Thomas, and, most influential, George Herbert Mead. No theorist has asserted this idea more vigorously than Herbert Blumer, the student of George Herbert Mead and the man who both coined the term symbolic interaction and was long the dominant exponent of symbolic interactionism as theory of society and human action. Blumer wrote:

> The prevailing practice of psychology and sociology is to treat social interaction as a neutral medium, as a mere forum for the operation of outside factors. Thus psychologists are led to account for the behavior of people in interaction by resorting to elements of the psychological equipment of the participants—such elements as motives, feelings, attitudes, or personality organization. Sociologists do the same sort of thing by resorting to societal factors such as cultural prescriptions, values, social roles, or structural pressures. Both miss the central point that human interaction is a positive shaping process in its own right. The participants in it have to build up their respective lines of action. As participants take account of each other's acts, they have to arrest, reorganize, or adjust their own intentions, wishes, feelings, and attitudes; similarly, they have to judge the fitness of norms, values, and group prescriptions for the situation being formed by the acts of others. Factors of psychological equipment and social organization are not substitutes for the interpretative process; they are admissible only in terms of how they are handled in the interpretative process. (Blumer 1969, p. 66)

Blumer's statement is, essentially, an elaboration of George Herbert Mead's presentation of the concept of emergence:

> Practically, of course, the novel is constantly happening and the recognition of this gets its expression in more general terms in the concept of emergence. Emergence involves a reorganization, but the reorganization brings in something that was not there before. . . . In a society there must be a set of common organized habits of response found in all, but the way in which individuals act under specific circumstances gives rise to all of the individual differences

which characterize the different persons. The fact that they have to act in a certain common fashion does not deprive them of originality. The common language is there, but a different use of it is made in every new contact between persons; the element of novelty in the reconstruction takes place through the reaction of the individuals to the group to which they belong. (Mead 1934, p. 198)

The contrast between Freud and the symbolic interactionist views of Mead and Blumer with regard to the concept of emergence could hardly be more dramatic. To Freud, sameness and latent pasts were more important than emergence. To Mead and Blumer, every new human interaction brings a reorganization, an emergence of novelty . To the psychoanalyst , the adult patient is unconsciously interpreting situations through a lens left over from childhood, and the psychoanalyst must learn how to interpret these patient interpretations. To Mead and Blumer, new interpretations are demanded by each interaction and each situation a person is in. A life course is constantly emerging in novelty, not reenacting childhood experience. And yet, what is one to make of Blumer's comment later in the same essay quoted above: " Social action, since it has a career, is recognized as having a historical dimension which has to be taken into account in order to be adequately understood" (Blumer 1969, p. 77)?

To paraphrase Mead, a life course consists of individualized social actions, concatenated in one person's lifetime. Each has a historical dimension. Might not some of them lead as far back as childhood? Does Blumer's formulation grant that some understanding of the experienced life course of a man in his forties is contributed by knowing something of his childhood experiences? One begins to think that what initially seemed a sharp polarization between Freud's and the Mead-Blumer view of emergence is not as profound as it first appeared. To be sure, as Guy Swanson once wrote, in a source I cannot now locate, "It is evident that Mead and Freud had quite different aspects of behavior at the center of their attention" (Swanson 1967, p. 29), and the present discussion in no way implies otherwise. But it does argue that the historical dimension accorded to social action in Blumer's formulation adds complexity and qualification to the concept of emergence. A life course is not simply a process of emergence. There are threads of continuity. The apparent polarity between Freud and Mead constituted for me a puzzle that has led me, in Part III, to a novel conceptualization of the relationship between childhood and adulthood. But in true symbolic interactionist fashion, my study of Tony Santangelo's life history propelled me beyond this puzzle into analyses that I did not anticipate beforehand.

A second puzzle engaged me as well. The lack of optimism that Rieff notes in Freud has a counterpart in sociological analyses of the working class. Working-class people have a hard life. S. M. Miller provided a capsule summary of their difficulties in an early paper. In addition to a high rate of unemployment, their life is marked by "low wages, their inadequate housing . . . the poor schooling offered their children, the neglect of public services in their neighborhoods, the frequent callousness of the police and welfare departments, their bilking by merchants—in short their second-class economic and political citizenship . . ." (Miller 1964a, p. 9). In another paper, he identified four different categories of working-class people: the stable poor, the strained, the copers, and the unstable (Miller 1964b). These are surely four variations on a theme of misery. Later studies by Sennett and Cobb (1973), Rubin (1976), and Howell (1984) add to the picture of hardship, pain, and dismal life. When these accumulated and convergent accounts of working-class life are considered alongside Mead's concept of emergence and novelty—which offers optimistic as well as pessimistic prospects—interesting questions arise. How does a working-class man maneuver in hardscrabble conditions? What does he see as constraints? What does he see as opportunities? What choices does he have? At what points in the life course do choices appear? Are there chinks in the wall of constraint? What does it take to get through them to the other side?

My two puzzles are parts of the same larger puzzle, which constitutes the central issue of this study and which I see as one of the central issues of the life course. My concern is with the issue of constraint and agency over a life course, as perceived and interpreted by a man who must make some kind of sense of his life as he has lived it, lives it now, and expects to live it. As the literatures of both working-class life and structural approaches to the life course imply, this life is subject to certain probabilities. The life history gets us as close as we are able to get to seeing how a man deals with those probabilities over the lifetime he has lived up to the time of recounting in early middle age, how he has concatenated his experiences into an experienced life course.

NOTES

1. One category of exception to the general prominence and celebrity of autobiographers is the national autobiography competitions conducted in Poland, Finland, and other East European and Scandinavian countries (Denzin 1989, pp. 59–60).

2. The minimum wage in 1974 was $2 per hour. *Statistical Abstract of the United States*, 1994. National Data Book, Table 669, "Effective Federal Minimum Hourly Wage Rates: 1950–1993 (Washington: U.S. Government Printing Office, 1994).

3. For a fascinating account and analysis of how collection of life histories from delinquents became a widespread activity see James Bennett, *Oral History and Delinquency* (Chicago: University of Chicago Press, 1981).

4. Notice must be taken that a life history obtained at a particular point in time yields what may be called a *currently available biography*. Cohler (1982) takes the view that a person's "personal narrative" of his life is continually changing, but he cites no studies that document and support his view. One may speculate that the

available biography may be more or less coextensive with the available biography that might be produced at another point in time. One may also speculate that some of the constitutive elements (events, judgments, etc.) produced in any given recounting would recur in subsequent recountings, so that these more or less stable elements of narrative may be thought of as constituting the person's *governing biography*, his experienced life course that endures through temporal change. The length of the temporal interval between discrete recountings would be a factor in the degree of continuity and change, as would be the occurrence of experiences that were of major interpretive significance to the recounter. Unless two or more life histories at different times are produced by the same person(s), we can have no firm conviction about how much a person's available biography changes from one time to another. The currently available biography is what we have to work with.

Not long ago I encountered an African American student who had taken a course with me a year or two previously. I said hello and was about to greet him by name when he announced a Muslim name, which was different from the very Anglo-Saxon name by which he was known when he was in my class. Clearly, I could infer that there had been a major change in his experienced life course. If I had been fortunate enough to have obtained two recountings of his life history, one at the time I first knew him and one since he changed his name, I would undoubtedly have discovered some important elements in the second that were not present in the first. But it is by no means certain that one could not find a stable governing biography in the two successive available biographies, along with new experiential elements. Without the material, the question is undecidable.

PART II

Tony Santangelo's Life History

INTRODUCTION: QUESTIONS TO A LIFE HISTORY NARRATIVE

The study of the human life course is a far-flung, multi-faceted enterprise conducted by scholars in sociology, psychology, human development, anthropology, gerontology, history, psychoanalysis, and women's studies, and it has been taken up by the recently emergent field of men's studies. The life history is a significant method in that enterprise. Like every research method, it raises certain questions. The reader about to embark on Tony Santangelo's life history may find it useful if I briefly mention some—both methodological and substantive—that seem to me especially important. The first two questions arise from my reading of another life history.

In the introduction to his life history of Tuhami, a tilesetter in Morocco, Vincent Crapanzano writes:

> The life history, like the autobiography, presents the subject from his own perspective. It differs from autobiography in that it is an immediate response to a demand by an Other and carries within it the expectations of that Other. It is, as it were, doubly edited: during the encounter itself and during the literary (re)-encounter. Not only do the specific questions posed by the Other reflect certain generic expectations within his own culture, but the very question of life history itself may be an alien construct for the subject and cause in him an alienating *prise de conscience*. The frequent elimination of the Other, at least in the form of a narrative I, renders the life history timeless and static. Ironically, this elimination of the I in the name of objectivity would totally preclude clinical and cultural evaluation were it not that the voice of the Other sounds through its own self-expurgated text. (Crapanzano 1980, pp. 8–9)

Two different main questions are implied here: (1) In what ways do my cultural expectations shape the life history that Tony Santangelo produced?

The life history was obtained from an American working-class man by an American scholar of lower middle class origin who has been moderately mobile into the upper middle class. Would a scholar of working-class background have obtained a different life history? Would a scholar whose culture and education were Japanese, or Kenyan, or Brazilian have obtained a different life history because of his specific culture and education? There is no clear and obvious answer to this question, but it is one the reader may want to ponder. (2) As noted in Part I in relation to another of Crapanzano's writings, the Other has not been eliminated in the present work. My questions and comments are reproduced unedited, and the reader is free to judge their impact as well as to witness my mistakes and, I hope, benefit from them. Perhaps there are points where I interrupted Tony to clarify something for myself when I would have done better to remain silent. Perhaps there are places where I should have probed further with follow-up questions. How does this particular interviewer—or life historian, if I may propose that designation for practitioners of this method (to take its place alongside statistician, demographer, ethnographer, clinician)—influence the life history that Tony Santangelo produced? The presence of the Other is not hidden or disguised in this work. What is its impact?

Crapanzano's writing produces additional relevant questions.

> Tuhami responded to our encounter . . . with an ease of fantasy and self-reference. It was often impossible to distinguish what was real from what was dream and fantasy, hallucination and vision. His interest was not in the informative but in the evocative aspect of language. He contradicted himself so often that even the minimum order I bestow on his life belies its articulation. (Crapanzano 1980, p. 14)

Again, this passage raises two main questions: (1) What is real and what is fantasy in Tony's life history? Is his language informative or is it other than informative? More generally, are statements made in life histories less truthful than answers to survey questions? A few pages earlier, Crapanzano referred to "the absolute distinction between the *imaginary* and the *real* that has dominated Western thought. The imaginary—the product of unconstrained desire at its limit—is relegated to a status inferior to that of the real, which parades under the standard of truth. The problem of what is or is not real is left to the philosopher. To Everyman, the real is both distinct from the imaginary and at one with the truth" (Crapanzano 1980, p. 7; italics in original). What standard of truth shall we use when we read and seek meaning in Tony Santangelo's life history? (2) How does Tony contradict himself and how does that affect our understanding of his life? I detect one important contradiction. At one point Tony claims that his drinking with buddies after work helps build goodwill and helps with getting construction jobs. At another point he says his work comes from the union, which suggests that there is a prescribed procedure and that drinking with men who are in other construction trades than his own contributes no advantage in getting work assignments. I discuss this contradiction in Part III. Are there other contradictions that I missed?

Different researchers approach the life course with different questions. For example, a central question for Glen Elder has been how historical change influences changes in the life course. For me, a central question has been—How are the different parts or phases or times of a life course connected? When Clifford Shaw's (1930) classic *The Jack-Roller* was reissued, Howard S. Becker wrote in a new introduction:

> The life history, more than any other technique except perhaps participant observation, can give meaning to the overworked notion of *process* . . . Social process . . . is not an imagined interplay of invisible forces or a vector made up of the interaction of multiple social factors, but an observable process of symbolically mediated interaction . . . [T]he life history, if it is done well, will give us the details of that process whose character we would otherwise only be able to speculate about. . . . It will describe those crucial interactive episodes in which new lines of individual and collective activity are forged, in which new aspects of the self are brought into being. (Becker 1966, pp. xiii–xiv)

To my mind, in this discussion Becker raises one of the important questions about a life course—How are new aspects of the self brought into being?—but neglects its complement. His comment overlooks or assumes away the possibility that there may be some continuities in the self over time. The ancient Greek philosopher Heraclitus said that one cannot step into the same river twice, that all is flux. But do all crucial interactive episodes lead to new aspects of the self that displace earlier aspects or can they sometimes add new aspects to ongoing aspects? Can there be both continuity and change in the self? Since adults have experiences that children and adolescents do not have, experiences that change them, does it matter what kind of childhood and adolescence a person has? Why would it matter if one is changing all the time, or changing in crucial interactive episodes? Is there any relationship between Tony Santangelo as a middle-aged adult and Tony Santangelo in his childhood and adolescent years? Are there processes of continuity as well as of change? While it may be easy to spot life-course change in response to historical change, can we spot continuity of self that persists through that change? Is all change alike? Or should we distinguish between changes *of* life course and changes *within* life course?

Finally, we may raise the question of whether adolescence is a fundamental and decisive period in the life course, at least a life course in the United States. Two very distinguished life-course scholars have, in different ways, made the case that it is. Erik Erikson, the only theorist to attempt a systematic theory of the whole life course from birth to the final years of life, delineated a series of eight life stages, each marked by a salient issue that is most pressing at that stage. The issue for adolescence he called "identity vs. role confusion" (1950). Adolescence is the period when the tentative formations of childhood are sorted out; when successful, the person is prepared to take on the tasks of adulthood. Erikson writes:

> All through childhood tentative crystallizations take place which make the individual feel and believe (to begin with the most obvious aspects of the matter) as if he approximately knew who he was—only to find that such self-certainty ever again falls prey to the discontinuities of psychosocial development. (1980, p. 122)

He goes on to say that

> [T]he process of identity formation emerges as an *evolving configuration*—a configuration which is gradually established by successive ego syntheses and resyntheses throughout childhood; it is a configuration gradually integrating *constitutional givens, idiosyncratic libidinal needs, favored capacities, significant identifications, effective defenses, successful sublimations, and consistent roles.* (1980, p. 125; italics in original)

Erikson then poses a question:

> The final assembly of all the converging identity elements at the end of childhood (and the abandonment of the divergent ones) appears to be a formidable task: How can a stage as "abnormal" as adolescence be trusted to accomplish it?

He answers that

> [A]dolescence is not an affliction but a *normative crisis,* i.e. a normal phase of increased conflict characterized by a seeming fluctuation in ego strength, and yet also by a high growth potential. (1980, p. 125; italics in original)

In a provisional summing up, he concludes: "I shall use the bare term 'identity' in order to suggest a social function of the ego which results, in adolescence, in a relative psychosocial equilibrium essential to the tasks of young adulthood" (1980, p. 161).

Starting from a very different intellectual perspective and traveling a different intellectual route, John Clausen arrived at a conclusion that is very close to Erikson's. In his major study, *American Lives,* Clausen (1995) developed his key explanatory concept, adolescent planful competence, and came to his major conclusion that

> [A]n adolescent's competence by the end of the high school years and the antecedents that gave rise to it strongly influence the direction that the life course will take, the ease of major transitions, and the person's success in performing the major roles that will be enacted over much of the life course. (1995, p. 16; italics in original)

When two such distinguished scholars of the life course have identified adolescence as so crucial for the life course, the question must be posed here: Did Tony's choices as an adolescent decisively shape his life course as he tells it at age forty-seven? There are, to be sure, some complications in asking and attempting to answer this question. What Clausen defines as the life course leaves out some matters that I consider essential to it, so that the definition of life course must be taken into account as the reader attempts to arrive at an answer. There are also differences between Clausen's and Erikson's approaches. Clausen explicitly says that he does not delve deeply into unconscious motivations (1995, p. 15), whereas Erikson is a psychoanalyst who does delve deeply into unconscious motivations.

These questions may be useful for the reader who may come to this document with no more than a general question: What should I be looking for as I read a life history? But every approach to the life course is a partial one, and the reader may bring his or her own questions to the life history.

THE LIFE HISTORY

Interview # I
Interview with Francis Anthony Santangelo
by Gerald Handel

Mr. Santangelo: My name is Francis Anthony Santangelo. Everybody calls me Tony. I was born February 19, 1927. I come from Italian parents. My mother was born in New York, but her mother was born in Genoa, Italy. My father was born in Chinatown on the Lower East Side. His folks were born in Parma, Italy. So I'm really what they call more or less of an Italian-American.

I was brought up in the Yorkville section of New York. I went to school, Catholic School, Our Lady of Good Counsel on East 91st Street which was two blocks away from my home. I also went to church there. My mother and father were married in that parish. I was christened there, communion, confirmation; I ended up graduating from that parish. In later years I was even married there, and my children were christened in that parish, so you can see I'm really a native Yorkville man.

I did eight years of grammar school. We lived at ____ Third Avenue, which is between 89th and 90th Street on Third. I graduated 1940. I forgot to mention, I have a brother whose name is Anthony and he was known as Big Tony and I was known as Little Tony. I idolized my brother. He was a great athlete. He was ten years older than I am. But I didn't really know him the way brothers more or less are normally close to each other, because the war had a big effect on our lives.

My brother was drafted a year before Pearl Harbor, and he did five years. He went away January 1941. I went away April 1945. He was still overseas when I was going into the service. I did two years in the service. Ended up like occupation duty in Japan. I was discharged late December 1946.

When I came out of the Army, my brother was home, and he was getting engaged, that meant I would be the only one at home. My father was working with his brother in a bar called Santangelo's Restaurant, which was a well-known Yorkville establishment. My grandfather opened it up in 1933, right after Prohibition, and they built it up into a very, very respectable steak house and eaterie, and very neighborhood place to go, you know, families, really a family place.

My father worked there as a night bartender, and I didn't see my father much because of the hours, so mostly my mother brought me up.

Like I say, my father was a bartender for his brother, and he was a heavy drinker. I guess his drinking did affect our lives, in the way of income into the house. I mean, don't get me wrong, we always ate and had shoes on our feet, but I think things could have been a little more comfortable if, like, he would have cut down a little bit.

My father died at 67 years old, by the way, of cirrhosis of the liver and hepatitis, which was caused from his drinking. But he was really a good guy. He was well liked in the neighborhood. Everybody knew him. His name was Jimmy. And he had a lot of friends. He was good to me. I guess I was his favorite because I was the youngest, you know. I really miss him at times. I was his biggest, I don't know, gleam in his eye, I guess, because I also became sort of an athlete of the neighborhood here, and became famous, so to speak, in the neighborhood circles as a ballplayer.

Well, I did three years—let's see, after I graduated, I went to Benjamin Franklin High School. I did two and a half years up there. I started to get away from schoolwork. I don't think it was the crowd I hung out with, it's just I guess I wasn't the type for it.

My mother and father were very upset about me quitting school. They said, "You're never going to get any place without an education" and they gave me the whole bit, and at the time, we all think we know what we're doing, but it proved later on of course that they were right. My brother in the meantime was getting ready to get married. 1948 he got married. And then I knew I had to go to work because I mean, everybody had money and I didn't have any money.

So a friend of my father's offered me a job in the building line, working with the ladders, carrying steel for them. So I went to work in 1949, construction, laborer, doing everything, like picking up rods, taking them here—heavy work. Seven hours a day. The pay I think at that time was a lot of money, it was about $80 a week or $85 a week, you know, and it was who you know in them days that got you working. Like my father had a lot of friends. "Jimmy's son, take care of Jimmy, make sure his son works," you know. And I was a good kid, like I wasn't a drinker, and most of the construction men at that time were drinkers, but it didn't bother me, because I was too busy, like as soon as work was over, I'd have a stick in my hand or a ball or a glove, and I'd be down at the ballpark. This was my life, playing sports.

I always wanted to be somebody, but I just became, just like a neighborhood somebody. Although I had tryouts with the Brooklyn Dodgers in 1949, the New York Giants in 1950, and the Pittsburgh Pirates in 1950. But it was the same old story, "We'll call you," and I'm still waiting to hear from them. But I accepted it. Because I'm really not a big strapping fellow, I go about 5-7½, about 160 pounds, and this was like, you know, 26 years ago, and I still hold to 160 pounds, so I try to keep in the best shape as I can.

Well, the fifties—during the fifties, I just stayed working in the building line, and things got a little easier in the house, with me working and bringing in some money.

We got our first telephone in 1950, believe it or not, our first refrigerator in 1950. We had the old ice box. We lived in a tenement, a four-room house, railroad rooms, with the bathroom in the hall and the bathtub in the kitchen. You wanted to take a bath, everybody had to leave the kitchen and go in the other rooms.

You say to yourself, in 1950 they had places like this! I don't know what the rent was, but it couldn't have been more than $30 or $40 in them days.

But money, like I say, was tough. My father didn't make a million. But he did drink a lot and I think that's where a lot of it went. If he didn't drink, we probably could have had a little more luxury.

You tell your friends you didn't have a refrigerator till 1950, they laugh at you. It's unbelievable. Especially a telephone in them days.

So, me going to work, we even got a television set in a couple of years. And it was like bringing a little luxury into the house, making it a little easier on my mother, which had worked hard all her life, and my father—he never—he gave her a little rough time occasionally, like you know, just abuse, I mean, nothing, no physical or anything like that. But I think that was due to the drink and the aggravation of his job. If somebody gave him a hard time, he was the type that would probably bring it home and take it out on my mother. If my mother said something wrong, you know, he would jump all over her, and anything to pick a fight, just to get out of the house.

OK, you know, enough of that. So I continued working in the building line. And then I met my wife, Catherine, went with her for about a year, got married 1954. I left the building line in 1954 because it wasn't steady in them days. In the early fifties, like '53 and '54, there was not too many buildings going up, and I knew I needed a steady job and a steady income, so once again I turned to my father, who had offered me a job, I neglected to tell you, 1948, in the Department of Sanitation. No test, nothing, political reasons, you could get on in them days, a favor—it was a favor. I did not take the job, because it consisted of a 5½ day work week, which meant working half a day on Saturday, even though it was steady and all the benefits and everything like that. I did not take it.

So I went to work with—He got me a job with Hotpoint Electric, which is General Electric Co. up in Yonkers. We got married and we moved up to the Bronx, which wasn't far from the job. I had a car even, with some of the money I had left over from when I worked in the building line.

So I tried this new job. It was putting units into refrigerators. If a unit burned out, we would be called and carry the unit into the building and hook up the unit. But it really wasn't my cup of tea. I wasn't happy. The money was way under what I was making in the building line, and I talked it over with my wife and I said I would rather go back into the building line for a few dollars less, for a few dollars more, and if it rains of course you don't work in the building line where in this other business you work, you get five days pay.

But I got an offer from my father's brother who ran the bar, and he said that he would break me in to be a bartender or a waiter or anything, to keep the name of the family going in the neighborhood.

So I said, "I don't know." I said I'd give it a shot. So he said, "Just try it on a Saturday. You work from 12 to 5. You won't have to give up the other job. See if you like it."

So I went to work on Saturdays from 12 to 5. He paid me $2 an hour, which was $10, plus tips. Well, seeing that I was Jimmy's son, everybody liked me, and they liked Jimmy. I got more in tips than I was doing in salary. All the money came in, and it was good.

I talked to my wife. I told her I wasn't very happy up at General Electric, so she said, "Why don't you quit?"

So I ended up quitting, and I went to work with the restaurant, my uncle's business, where my father worked. I went in there. He was very (inaudible) before, and I started in Santangelo's Restaurant, Steak House it was, in 1956, early '56.

I used to work two days on the bar, at night. Monday and Tuesday I'd go to work at 6 o'clock at night and I'd work till 3 o'clock in the morning. Wednesday and Thursday, I was a waiter in the daytime. When I say daytime, I used to like work from 12 o'clock in the afternoon till 8 at night. Friday and Saturday, I was a bartender in the daytime, working from 8 in the morning till 5 at night. So I was working six days a week, and they were paying me at that time $80 a week—plus gratuities, which was mine, tips.

Things became a little easier with the steady work and the tips were really a help in them days, made the job. The salary wasn't big, because people were making like $140 and almost double what I was making, but I had the tips.

The restaurant in them days was 85th Street and First Avenue. We lived over the restaurant, the next adjoining building, so there was really no carfare at the time involved, and it had its conveniences. We could get food and everything like that. I didn't have to pay for my wife to come for dinner, the kids, a container of milk, anything like that. So things were starting to look up.

And then I became a steady day bartender. They took me off of waiting and everything. In the meantime, my first child came along. She was born in 1955,

Nancy. I was working as a day bartender. Now I'm up to $125 a week plus gratuities, working six days a week. Earning is fine. I'm playing my ball. I'm very happy. We even have a car. My son James is born 1958, named after my father.

We moved now from 85th Street and First Avenue to 93rd Street and Second Avenue. Better apartment, steam heat, would you believe, getting steam heat in 1959? Nobody would believe that in this day and age, but I didn't have steam heat till 1959.

We had box rooms up there. We were very happy. We were still in the neighborhood. All our friends were here. Her mother was living down the block. My mother lived four blocks away. I stayed in the bar, still working. My other daughter is born. 1966. Marie. Everything is fine. Still working in the bar.

The owner of the bar dies. No, excuse me—my father dies. My father dies. From the hepatitis, from drinking. He's told to take it easy. He started to take it easy in the last six or seven months of his life but it was too late, because it had already turned his skin to jaundice like. He was yellow. He was on strict diet and everything like that. He couldn't work any more, and it was just more or less eating at him.

My mother is still alive. God bless her. She lives by herself. My uncle paid for his funeral—the least he could have done, he worked 27 years for him—and made it a little easier on my mother.

My mother—the place goes on as business. Business is great, but my salary remains the same. These relatives don't want to give you a dime. They believe in you working for what you get in life, you know, that's the way they go. And they're very tough people to work for. Even though I'm making money, they don't give you a pat on the back or any way, you know. They give me like two weeks vacation and make sure you're back, you know, and all this. Very strict people to work for. The boss dies, three years after my father, the owner. He leaves the place to his brother, his younger brother, who is 18 years older than me. Great mind for the business, but a horrible man for handling people.

They have to get out of their location, which they've been there for 35 years in one spot, and like I say it was a landmark. They move to Second Avenue between 84th and 85th Street which is one block west from their original location. Business takes a big nosedive. Whether it's the move, whether it's the idea of the younger brother taking over, I don't know what it was, but I mean, I carried my weight, because my friends were in a different era, younger, and their wives used to come and see me when I worked on the bar and everything like that. But for some reason or other, he falls into debt and he's trying to sell the place.

1973, January 13, he has a heart attack right on the premises, and he drops dead.

My salary right now is up to $165 a week, plus gratuities again. In the past two years he has made me night manager, which more or less has kept me away from my family, and my wife resents it. She tells me to get out of the job and I say, "Where am I going to go at this stage of life?"

It's late now. Maybe I will get the business.

And I did get the business, in more ways than one. I thought I would get the steak house, but my cousins, the boss's daughters, sell the place right out from underneath me, and I'm out in the cold.

Sensing that this was going to happen, three years prior, a friend of mine who was in construction business, in the ironworkers end, offers me a job to see if I would be interested in going back into the construction business, but a different end of it.

I said, "All right, I'll try it." So I went back and naturally, the figures today or a year ago or three years ago are fantastic in the building line. You work seven hours a day, 35 hours a week, you come home, you walk away from your job, you have no headaches, whereas when you're running the bar as a manager, you have to wonder who's coming through the door, are you going to get stuck up? Are you going to have to fight somebody who's drunk, break up a quarrel between a man and a wife, anything like that?

I accept his offer, and I go to work for him for three weeks. I like it. I fill out an application to become an ironworker. The application comes through two years later and I become a full-fledged ironworker, and this is what I'm doing today.

But just getting back to that holdup bit, as I'm thinking now—seven years ago, I'm closing up the place. It was on Labor Day weekend, and I'm just about to get into my car. I get into my car and I ride to where I live, 93rd. Got out of my car and I'm walking up toward my house, and two men walk up behind me.

I see the two men. I turn around. I say, "Well, maybe they're going into the same building I am, just one of those things." But seeing it's 3 o'clock in the morning, and being the little cagey fellow I am, I don't trust anybody. I walk through the doorway and into the yard, to see if they would follow, and sure enough, when I turned around to see if they were following, they're right behind me, and they got on each side of me and said, "Don't run," and they called me by my name, Tony.

Well, that's not too odd because all you had to do was come into the bar in them days and if you just stayed there and had two drinks, you would know who Tony was because everyone used to say, "Hello, Tony, what's new? Who won? The Yankees?" and all this. I was very sports minded. And I would talk.

Anyway, they took me back to the place and said, "No, you're not going to get hurt. Your wife's not going to get hurt. We have somebody watching her."

Well, as soon as they threatened my wife and family, I completely complied with what they wanted. I went back to the bar. We had a night watchman there. His name was Jack. He saw me. He let me in, but he didn't see the two fellows, they were on the side of the door. He let us in. They tied him up. They asked me to get the receipts and the money from the register where I'd put it. It was a long weekend. It was a Sunday night. We had Friday night's receipts,

Saturday night's receipts, and Sunday night's receipts, plus the payroll for the help which consisted of about eight people.

They got roughly around $4,700 that night, and there was two of them, like I say. One wasn't bad. One was very nice. There was one there was very jittery. He was the man I was afraid of.

So we left the place. They had the money. We got back in my car, and we drove to my house, with the two of them alongside. I was driving. One was in the back seat and one was alongside of me. They said, "Just drive normal, get to your house, no one's going to get hurt."

So I got to the house. I said I wanted to know about my wife. They said, "Don't worry about it, when we leave here, your wife will be all right, promise." So they parked on the East River Drive by 92nd Street by the ASPCA. The nice fellow got out with the money, and evidently had a car around 93rd Street a half a block away. The fellow I was afraid of stayed in the car.

Now, at that time in the morning, he could have shot me ten times and nobody would have heard nothing and I would have been just found in the morning. So I really didn't know what to do. I was very tempted to just make an attempt to overpower him, and then for some reason, the threat on my family had kept me completely more or less calm and not to do anything. But he got out of the car just after a minute; I guess it was just to give his partner time to get into the car, warm it up or whatever it was, and he told me, "You drive down York Avenue and go back to the place and untie your porter and call the police," just like that. So I knew that I was dealing with fellows who knew what they were doing, even though one of them was nervous.

So I went back and I did that, I took a drink myself, because I was shaking like a leaf, called the police department. They came. We had known some of the police in the area from coming in and having dinner and stuff like that. And they said that I was very lucky because they were definitely professionals. Seeing that they picked me up at my house and drove to the place of business, which was only seven blocks, eight blocks away, but stayed with me like for forty minutes to get the money and then drove you back to the place and then left.

He said, "But of course, the whole thing about having your wife held was completely a hoax." They didn't do that.

At that time, like I say, my wife was pregnant with my daughter, my youngest daughter. She was eight months pregnant and I was really concerned about her. So I guess that slows you up a little bit, you know.

So here I am today, working in the building line, and making very reasonable amount of money. It's comfortable. The only bit is, if it rains you don't work and you don't get paid. My daughter is 18. She's working. My son is in high school, and my little baby is three years in grammar school.

I don't know where to go from there, Gerry.

Q: OK, that's fine. I don't know whether we got down—You mentioned something about your relationship with your father before, but we didn't get it down on the tape. Would you mention that again? Let's go back, tell me about your relationship with your parents when you were real young.

Santangelo: Well, like I say, my mother brought me up mostly, because my father worked in the bar and his hours conflicted more or less. He was a night worker. Went to work around 4 o'clock in the afternoon and he worked till 3:30 in the morning. Now, when you're a kid and you go to school, you leave the house at 8:30 in the morning, your father's sleeping. And you come home at 3:30 from school, he's already gone to work. So I really only saw my father in the morning when he was sleeping. The only day I really seen him was having Sunday dinner before he went to work, I would see him, and then on Monday was his day off, and my father always came home like with a half a load on Monday.

Because he would make the rounds of the bars. All his friends used to come to see him and give him tips. And this was the game in them days. You had a drink here, and this bartender from 91st Street come to see you, the bartender from 90th Street would come and see you another night, and then when it was your day off you would go to see them. It was a game of just put and take.

Q: Give each other drinks.

Santangelo: Yes, they would give each other drinks and leave each other $2. It was a form of goodwill in those days. It was a form of goodwill—not that you had to do it, it was just something, it was your way of building up business too. "Look who came to see me, the bartender from five blocks away," you know. It was always good in the register. You know what I mean? And my father would do the same thing on his day off. He would go and see him and see that one and that one, and meanwhile, that money that he was spending of course could have made things a little easier for my family and myself. I mean, like I say, we always had shoes on our feet and food on the table, but we had no telephone. We had a cold water flat without steam heat. We had a bathroom—

Q: No heat at all?

Santangelo: We used to have a coal stove. Used to have the coal man up. We used to have to get a 15 and 20 cent piece of ice when we were kids. Used to have to dump the water from the ice pan underneath the ice box—I was going to say refrigerator—and I believe like, things could have been a little easier if he wasn't a bit of a drinker. But he—I mean, when I say he was a drinking man, the man always worked. He wasn't one of these types that didn't go to work on account of drink. Of course he worked in a place where the drink was there, so maybe that's what made him go to work, you know what I mean? But he used to stop drinking occasionally, you know what I mean, but he became a very irritable man when he didn't drink. He was a different person altogether. Like he was very liberal with his money when he was drinking. Like if I asked him for 50 cents when I was a kid, he would give me 75, you know what I mean? Yet if he wasn't drinking in them days and I asked him for 50 cents I'd get a quarter. You know. My mother could never get an extra dime out of him, like for the house, for little—to make things easier. Could never get nothing out of him.

Like I say, a well-liked man in the neighborhood, very well-liked man. But it's a shame.

Q: His brother owned the restaurant.

Santangelo: Right.

Q: Whose was it—their father?

Santangelo: That's right. The reason why he never got partnership in that restaurant was mainly because of his drinking. They could not rely on him. He was there. He worked every day. But they could not rely on him. They were afraid that if they gave him any power, he would give the place away. He had too many friends. Like if you came in or I came in and we weren't working, you could put a dollar on the bar and stay five hours. He was like that. He knew. But he made—there was goodwill, friendship—not only friendship, but later on people never forgot that. They came back. And I'm talking about doctors from Doctors Hospital who were interns then. They could always come up there, and if they were broke, my father would always carry them without his brother knowing it. In other words, they never forgot Jimmy. They never forgot him. And he always knew what it was to be broke. He never shunned anybody. Like I've seen men down on their feet come into the bar, like I guess you'd call them bums from the Bowery, you know, that just drift around, and they would say, they wanted a dime or a quarter for a drink, and my father would say, "You're not going to get that, but if you want something to eat, I'll gladly give you something." And he would never turn anybody away in that respect if they were hungry. For a drink, he would never give it. It's a funny thing, he would never give them money, but he always offered them drinks. Something to eat, I mean. And I've already seen him take his coat off the wall, his overcoat, and give it to a man on a bad night that was cold out. The guy was really in bad shape, and he had no coat on, it was snowing and everything like that—just sounds like something really farfetched, but he took his coat off and he gave it to the guy. He had a great heart, my father.

Q: Where's your brother now?

Santangelo: My brother works for the telephone company in New York City. He works in the UN. He's special representative for the company, handles some accounts down there. Tony got married, Big Tony I'll say got married in 1948. He's got three lovely children. One is married, two are in high school. One is going to be a senior this year, and the other one is in second year high.

Tony had a bad heart attack 12 years back. It shook up our family, my father, my mother, of course. Here's a man who was in great condition and 40 years old. He had a very severe heart attack, and they took him to Booth Memorial which is out on Long Island, and the doctor they had I believe—it was just a family doctor, general doctor, not a heart specialist, and my uncle was alive at the time, and he volunteered, if it was OK with my brother's wife, to let his heart doctor go out and see Tony and he would pay for it. The man's name was Dr. Malden, who wrote I think a couple of books on the heart a few years back.

I drove Dr. Malden out to the hospital that night. There was a big hustle and bustle about another doctor coming in on the case and everything like that, but I didn't want to know anything; it was my brother, he was in bad shape, and they finally consented when they found out where his [Dr. Malden's] credentials were. New York Hospital, Medical Center, all these big names, so he was well known and they let him look at my brother.

On the way back from Booth Memorial that night, this Dr. Malden told me that my brother had a very very severe cardiac arrest, that his heart was like soft oatmeal mush; it was—it had pierced the heart. He said the medication they were giving him was not strong enough, because if they gave him too much you could stop the heart, and he was explaining different things. But to this day I believe that this man saved my brother's life.

My brother was in the hospital seven months with that heart attack. He was out of work 11 months, but being with the phone company so long, they carried him on full pay for half a year, and then they put you on half pay, half week's pay or whatever it is you know for the second half.

It's funny that we should mention my brother because this is February, and in December he just had another heart attack, after 14 years. 12 or 14 years ago. Right now, he had it in December, but he's home now, and he's not allowed to go to work yet. They're building him up again. It's funny, that heart patient—this disease strikes at anybody. Like his wife says he doesn't know how to relax. My wife says that's all I do is relax. It's such a big thing. Like, everything bothers my brother. He worries about, if his kid is supposed to be home at 9, if it's 10 after 9—little things. Where I don't have that attitude, see. Maybe I should. But he's really a great guy. He doesn't smoke. He doesn't drink. He does everything right down to the book, and here it is, getting stricter with something like that, where a guy like me you'd figure would get it, the guy that does anything.

Q: Let's go back to your childhood. I'd like to see you remember as much as you can about your childhood, from as early back as you can. You know, give as much detail as you can about your childhood.

Santangelo: Family and everything?

Q: Everything about your childhood.

Santangelo: OK. I guess I can go back to about when I was three, four years old. My father like I say was working. Just started to work in the bar in those days. Prohibition was then—it was about '33, it was. My mother was working someplace, I really don't know where. She used to leave me with her mother. And I used to cry like anything, because my grandmother was watching me and I was a real mother's boy in them days. No one could leave me alone with anybody. I was a real pain in the neck.

Then I remember, my mother stopped working a few years later. We were on Third Avenue at the time. I don't know, as a kid I got everything I wanted. When I was 9, 10, 11 years old I used to read comic books and I used to have ice cream. As bad off as my family was and my mother was, they never neglected to give me anything. They always found a way. I don't know what it was. I think, if my father had a good day on the bar or something like that he would always, you know, throw me an extra nickel or dime in them days.

Like I say, I was very interested in sports. I played an awful lot of sports when I was a kid. I wasn't the greatest scholar in school. But I was never a bad boy like at home to my mother. I was a spoiled brat, but I'd never do nothing—if she called me, I would come, you know, stuff like that. I used to accompany her to the movies at night because my father couldn't take her out at night. I remember that well, because my father used to get a pass to the RKO, and it was good for any night during the week, not on weekends. It was good for Monday to Thursday nights. And the shows in them days used to change during the week, and my mother would take me. The pass was good for two, and I used to accompany my mother to the show. Of course, my brother was old enough to be going out with girls and I was only a kid. As I said, there's ten years difference between me and my brother.

But my mother really didn't have much of a social life, for going out at night. On occasion, my father would always invite her down to the bar on the weekend, to come down and see her friends. She knew everybody my father knew. And she wasn't much of a drinker. She would maybe take two drinks a night. And it's a funny thing, she used to take me. I used to go with her everyplace, when I was seven, eight years old. I used to go to a bar on a Saturday night with her, and all the people at the bar used to give me nickels to play the pinball machine, and she used to tell me, "Put them in your pocket, save it for ice cream in the morning."

But we'd sit there, and she'd talk to her friends, and I would just drink Coca-Cola and eat cherries and play the machine all night, that was my mother's big night out. Then on Sunday she would ride up to see her mother, who had lived in the Bronx and I would go and accompany her there. I used to do all these things, until I just got around to get on my own, you know, go places by myself. I always went everyplace with my mother. I guess I was like a steady companion. Of course, my father never went hardly any place with her. He never seen a movie in his life, I think.

Q: How—why do you say you were a spoiled brat?

Santangelo: Well, I always got my own way.

Q: From your mother?

Santangelo: From my mother. Oh, my father would give me anything. Yet I had a fear about my father, put into me from my mother. She said to me, she used to get mad at me when I was bad or whatever I did to get in trouble, she used to go to the strap and try to take a couple of schwacks at me. I'd run under the bed. She'd say, "I'll tell your father when he comes home, " and she always told me a story that when my brother was young, and did something bad, that my father smacked him in the face and he had the imprint of his hand on his face for two days. And it really shook me up. I was deadly afraid of my father in that respect. I knew my father loved me, and I was the apple of his eye, but I never really wanted to get him angry at me. And he never really did get angry at me. Like I could twirl him around my finger. And he was a tough man, you know. He didn't care about anybody, like if he had a fight, he would fight anybody. It was his job. It was a rough job, being a bartender in the late thirties and forties. It was rough times and he had a lot of fights in bars and everything like that. But for some reason or other, like, I know I was the apple of his eye, and more or less my brother was of my mother. You know, like she—I hate to say the word favoritism. They loved us both and we loved them both. But I know I could get anything out of my father. Anything. And later on in life, my brother could too.

Later on in life. Not in the early part, I think. Later on in life, he—my father would do anything. If I told him I was playing ball, he would come and see me. He never did that for my brother, you know, when he was playing. He never called me by my name. He never called me Francis or anything like that. He used to call me the Kid. I was always the Kid to him. You know.

Q: How did you feel about that?

Santangelo: I felt it was a special name and I really enjoyed being called the Kid by my father. Yeah.

Q: What about the other kids when you were a kid? What was it like with you and other kids?

Santangelo: Well,—OK. Right. I grew up with a nice bunch of guys. There was the tough guy, the neighborhood tough guy we had. And we had the guy that was always—would always be stealing an apple, or going into a candy store and stealing candies, chewing gum: the guy that would go to the five and ten and steal something down there, anything, pair of socks to wear and everything like that.

Stealing was a funny thing in them days. Everybody did it. But there was a friend of mine, a good friend of mine who became a fighter. He was an amateur. He was very good as an amateur. We were the same age. I never seen a guy like, when he became of drinking age, get in more trouble like in bars. He was very good and he got a reputation, and it was just like in the days of the gunfighter years ago. The other neighborhood tough guy would come, and we'd all be in the bar, and he'd walk in and a fight would start and everything like that, you know. There'd be girls involved. It was a big crazy thing in them days.

I had a friend of mine was older than me—like I say, most of the fellows I grew up with were older than me, and I think this helped me an awful lot growing up, because I didn't really have that babyish thing about me when I was small. I always hung out with fellows like three or four years older than me. I was always the youngest one in the crowd. I believe it gave me the smarts—the experience, how to handle different situations, you know.

I know I was born with a sense, some sort of sense of reason to know when trouble was brewing, and I would stay away from it, like I never had anything to do with the police. I've never stolen anything—I mean, I'm not talking about an apple off a stand or a potato at the fruit market. I did that when I was a kid. We used to make a fire and throw the potatoes in the fire, and then we used to call them "hot mickies" in them days and eat them.

But I've never been in any trouble like that, yet some of my friends, like one was in a stickup of a gas station, and this was after the war. He had a hell of a war record. He was in Normandy. He was shot in the head. He lived to tell about it. Fortunately the bullet didn't go into his brain. But he came out, and after 1950 him and another fellow held up a gasoline station on 52nd Street and Tenth Avenue, and they were caught, and he—I think he just, he's coming up for parole, and this is going back, it must be almost 24 years ago. Of course, there was somebody killed in that. I think one of the attendants was shot, and the two of them that did it didn't admit who killed the person, so they both got like not life sentences but 40 years or whatever it was because there was a death involved. See, the guy had a wonderful war record, and he thought the world owed him a living for being in the service, and he didn't want to work.

You know, it's a funny thing—I believe that the service can either make a bum out of you or a man out of you sometimes. It all depends on how you look at it. Some guys come out, think the world owes them a living, the country owes them a living, "I'm not gonna do this, I'm not gonna do that, " and yet, it's no way to think. And a lot of my friends thought that way. This poor guy had 25, 26 years behind bars. For what? I mean, for nothing. His whole life is there, and he'll be getting out—

Another fellow I went to school with, the same thing. Him and three other fellows held up a candy store. And they beat the candy store man to death. Now, there was three of them involved and no one would admit who the guilty party was. But he came out. He's out three years now—the same age, we're a month apart in age. We graduated from the same grammar school. And you would never believe, if you saw us face to face, that this fellow is the same age as myself. He's stone grey, drawn, hard as nails—hard as nails, because his whole life has been behind bars, more or less, since he was a kid. He went away when he was 21 years old. And his whole life is behind bars. His mother died while he was in jail. And I think it was Elmira or Dannemora, one of those places upstate, and he had served 18 years, and they're giving him permission to come home for the funeral, and on the way down he tried to escape. And they caught him, and they put him right back on the train. They didn't even bring him down for the funeral or nothing; they put him back, they added another few years on his thing. And I can't understand what goes through these fellows' minds, like this. Out of respect for his mother—see, things like that. I don't have much respect for him. He's a friend of mine, I went to school with him—I know him, he's an acquaintance. All right, he did something wrong. He was involved in a crime. And they were giving him more or less of a two-day pass or a day pass to come down and see his mother, that he didn't see like in 12 years, before the poor woman was buried. You know, he had broken her heart, first of all by being caught in this crime and everything like that, and here he is—he jumps off a train and tries to get away, and they just added more years. I really lost a lot of respect for that man, you know.

But most of the other crowd was a good bunch of guys. They grew up, went on to jobs, I have a friend of mine who works for the government now. He just came back from Brussels. Has something to do with the cleaning(?) I don't really know what his job consists of, but he works in the PXs and things like that in the service, and he married a schoolmate of mine, Jean, and they're both New Yorkers but I think they're married like 23 years now and I think they've only lived in the States three years. They've been like [to] Tokyo in Japan and all over the country.

And then some of them are—When I played ball right after the war, I started to hang out with a different crowd of guys, from St. Ignatius—that's over on Park Avenue and 84th St.—and this was really a different group of fellows than I was normally known to hang out with, like, but the guys I was hanging out with were a little tough, like I say, they were fighters and everything like that. This was a different crew. They never thought anything like that. They were very sports-minded, and the guys I was with, some of them were sports-minded but not all of them. But this whole clique over here, they were my age—well, a year younger than me but they were well organized, and I went to Our Lady of Good Counsel—and St. Ignatius, they were rivals anyway. So I ended up playing with St. Ignatius, and I met a whole new group of fellows that were really like very instrumental in my life, like meeting people and everything like that. I met some nice people through these fellows, like one guy is retired policeman today, just went down to Florida. He's my age and he's retired. I laugh when I think of this, when I think back, my father wanted me to take that DS —I could have been—Department of Sanitation job—I could be retired today.

But he's retired today. He's down in Florida. There's another man, friend of mine, two of them I played ball with, are firemen. See, they all went for good jobs—insurance men—all ended up with the St. Ignatius crowd, they all ended up with good jobs. I don't know what it was, whether it was the difference in the neighborhoods, which were—which could be, because in them days, every block had its own gang. Today it's not that way. Today, because of the way the construction is and the building and hard-to-get apartments, everybody in a three-block area hangs out together. In those days, every block had its own gang, every block, and you had your own stickball team, you had your own softball team, your own baseball team. It was really funny. The best move I ever made was going with that St. Ignatius crowd, because in 1949 I remember we won Catholic Youth Organization Baseball League, and we won a trip to Battle Creek, Michigan.

Q: You played with St. Ignatius?

Santangelo: I played with St. Ignatius baseball team.

Q: You were out of high school then?

Santangelo: Oh yes, this is after the war now. This is after the war.

Q: St. Ignatius is what, a high school?

Santangelo: St. Ignatius is a grammar school. It's a parish.

Q: So it's a parish team. You're out of grammar school—

Santangelo: Right.

Q: You played with them even though that wasn't your parish?

Santangelo: Right.

Q: How did you happen to get in with them in the first place? How did you even go over there? What drew you over there?

Santangelo: Well, I lived at 90th Street and Third Avenue, and this fellow Charley Rooney lived across the street, and he went to St. Ignatius. And I went to Our Lady of Good Counsel and he used to say to me, "Why don't you come over and try out for our baseball team?"

When I say I played a lot of ball, I used to just go down and we used to choose up sides and organize. We'd have our own games.

He said, "Why don't you come over? I'll introduce you to some of the guys. Play ball for us; you're a good ballplayer."

So one Saturday I met him, and he took me over and introduced me to these fellows and the priest who was running the team, this Father O'Shea, and I tried out for the team and I had no trouble making it, and they were [a] much better organized club than what I was doing. I had no organization [at] all. They had uniforms. And—well, let me say something here. St. Ignatius is a very rich parish in New York City today, and in them days it was the second to St. Patrick's Cathedral. Like Jim Farley and the Kennedys and all these big Catholic names used to always go to that church on Sunday. And Our Lady of Good Counsel which is only six blocks away, but is on the other side of the tracks more or less, because St. Ignatius is on Park Avenue, Our Lady of Good Counsel is between Second and Third Avenue. So they had more of the so-called upper class people putting money in the baskets than we did.

So we had uniforms, we had everything over there. We had the best. Because I remember how we got our uniforms. Father O'Shea said, "We need uniforms. I'm going to make an announcement from the pulpit." And he made an announcement from the pulpit, saying that we have a team representing us now, they're going to go into the CYO, and the church cannot afford to give them any money toward this venture, and everything like that.

Do you know that three days later, he had an unsigned—he had a signed check and all he had to do was fill in the amount of the figure for the equipment? That meant uniforms, bats and balls and everything. I had never seen anything like this in my life. Because even when I was with the fellows, they said, "We're going down to Thorpes on Fifth Avenue for the uniforms."

Not down to, like we used to call it, "Jew Town," way downtown where you get everything in cheap, you know what I mean.

So they said, "We 're gonna go to Thorpes."

I said, "Are you kidding?"

He said, "We have the unsigned check. Father just fills it in. We get our uniforms."

And these guys weren't spoiled. They didn't take advantage of nothing. They really were a hell of a bunch of guys. And we ended up winning in '49 and went to Battle Creek—the nuns made us sandwiches, everything was on the house, we had lunch money out there. The situation was that we played in the Little World Series of 1949, representing New York City, New York State, I should say, and if we won—if you lost two games you were eliminated. Unfortunately, we were good, but we stepped out of our class going out there. We lost the first two games we played. We lost to Oklahoma and we lost to Ohio, and we were on the train four days later coming back to New York.

But it was an experience that I'll never forget. When you go someplace, that it's paid for, and guys who were working—I wasn't working at the time. I was laid off from the construction job, was in between jobs, so it made no difference to me, but some of the fellows had to take their vacations then, specially the fellows on the cops and the Fire Department, had to get leave of absence and get the OK that they were going on this trip. And even the priest from the parish flew up to see us play. For me it was beautiful. It was really something. And they were a hell of a bunch of guys.

They had a basketball team too, but I never played basketball. But I used to go watch them. They used to play in different tournaments all over the city.

Q: You mentioned some—Think back now over your life from the beginning till now, and tell me all the people who have been important to you, and the ways they've been important. You've mentioned some, but start going into that a little more in detail, and maybe there's somebody you didn't touch on. Who would you say were the important people in your life?

Santangelo: Well, I guess my brother is very big in my life. I think he set the stage for me to become interested in sports.

Q: Was he interested in sports?

Santangelo: Yes, my brother was a very good athlete. He played a lot of sports, yes. And I think it's what's around you and who's around you, more or less, that brings it out in you. I idolized my brother. Idolized him as a ballplayer. I wanted to do everything as good as him, and better, if I could. I really made a goal like of that, you know what I mean? I practiced and practiced to do things like that.

Like I can safely say and honestly say that if it wasn't for him, I don't know where—I might have been one of those fellows in that gas station. Something like that, who wasn't sports-minded, you know. Sports has an awful lot to do in the upbringing of a youth today. Even in them days, definitely, and even today. Because I ended up being coach, manager, later on for Our Lady of Good Counsel and St. Ignatius later on, in life. But my brother was very big in that, you know.

Let's see. Well, you forget, fellows that did things for you in them days, like getting your first uniform from a fellow named Joe Fanning who had a uniform. I never had a baseball uniform in my life. I used to play in dungarees and sneakers and a sports shirt. And I remember him saying to me, "Gee, I got a uniform, why don't you wear a uniform?"

I said, "I ain't got no uniform."

"I'll give you my uniform."

I said, "Yeah?"

He said, "Well, I don't use it no more. I'm finished."

He's married, you know, and—he gave me my first uniform. If you'll notice, everything like I'm talking about more or less pertains to sports, in the sports area. But—

Then other guys that also made an impression on me is the fellows that got in trouble. And I would stay away from these fellows. I knew that they're some fellows, like in the Li'l Abner cartoon, the little fellow with the cloud over his head—trouble always finds him. I don't know, it was like a sixth sense that used to tell me, "There's going to be trouble, don't go with them, down, you know tonight."

"Where you gonna go?"

"We're gonna go over to the Park."

They used to have Park dances over at the Mall in them days on Thursday nights; they used to have big name bands there for nothing. We used to go over there, there'd be other blocks—yes, over in Central Park—and there would be—fights would break out over girls. You know, "She's my girl," or his girl, and it made no difference to me 'cause girls didn't bother me. I was too busy playing sports. That's another story of my life, the girls.

Girls come into your life. You'd be surprised. Like I never really knew about girls. I knew what they were. But this—another thing, a girl is a big thing in my life. She came into my life when I was 16 years old. I was playing ball, and I never even took a girl home in them days. Today, they're taking them home when they're 13. But this girl come up to me and she says, "Do you like this girl?"

I said, "Yes, she's all right."

"Well, isn't there something about her that you like?"

I said, "I dunno, she goes with Gene, Gene Connolly over there. Why?" She said, "Yeah, but she wants to go with you."

Wants to go with me? I mean, where does she want to go? I didn't even know what going together meant, in them days, you know. I really wasn't interested in it.

But it was like anything else. She stopped going with this Connolly, and we started going together, and we were going together for about three years and she was the big thing in my life. She was my first love and everything like that.

Q: 16 when you started.

Santangelo: 16 and when I went in the service, I was going with her. When I was overseas, one of my best friends was going with her, and when I came back, she was engaged to marry my best friend. But it was the big thing in my life, like, you know. It was a big hurt, too. She had an important part to play in my life, my education, when it came to the females. More or less. You know. I got an education. I have a lot to thank with her. Even though she broke my heart at the time. Yeah.

Then I met a priest. Father Durney in Our Lady of Good Counsel parish, 15 years ago. I never met a man more understanding with people than he was. He was also interested in children and he wanted to do everything for kids, you know, and we got to talking. He liked the same things I did. He used to come into the restaurant and have dinner with me. We used to go to hockey games together. Dinner together. Outings together. We used to take kids with us, you know. He devoted his life more or less. He was a Catholic priest, but it's funny, in this area—he was driven out of this area by people.

Q: How do you mean?

Santangelo: When I say that, I mean they took him so much for granted. To let this parish be run by a woman, and not men. This is what happened to this man. He had to really run out of here to get away. He asked for a transfer. He'll never admit to this, but this is what really happened to this man. The teachers were making passes at him and everything like that. He was a good-looking man, you know what I mean? I believe he had his sneakers on. So, you know, even though we know that priests are getting married today, leaving the priesthood, you know—I just hope. I don't know, he's in love with God is the way I look at it and that's his life. But he went down to Tompkins Park Parish, down there by the Village, tough parish, lot of narcotics and everything like that. They broke in and stole his TV down there. They did everything to this man. They stole his battery from his car. And this is what he wanted, to get close to these people. He speaks Spanish. Get their respect, the underprivileged people. But here he was very happy, had everything going for him, because in the parish up here, three meals a day—down there he was eating TV dinners.

He was a big thing in my life. He's a very great personal friend of mine today in fact, you know.

Q: You still see him.

Santangelo: I'm ashamed of myself, I owe him a phone call right now, I should be talking to him.

Q: But you stay in touch.

Santangelo: Yes. Well, to tell you the truth, since the restaurant is gone—he used to come in at least once every two weeks. Not to see me, but bring different people in who had problems, and he used to sit with them in the booth and have dinner and talk them out. Young people, old people, black people, Spanish people, all walks of life. Man had a heart as big as his body. And if he stuck around, I'd sit down with him, have a drink or two, converse with him and maybe make an appointment with him to go to a game together or something like that. But we've really been out of touch since the place is gone. Now, the place is gone six months now. It's not fair to him and to myself to be this far apart. We have to get together for dinner. He's really a well-known man in this neighborhood, really well known. Yeah. Great man. Young fellow, too. Younger than myself, may I add.

Q: Who are the other people who are important in your life now?

Santangelo: Well, my wife. My children. I have friends, I have acquaintances, you know, good friends—they're all part of me more or less, but naturally my wife is everything. My kids. I want the best for my kids. I have an awful lot of friends, and it's a funny thing, I've said this a thousand times—I only had one brother. I never had a sister. But when I got married in 1954 if I didn't have a brother to pick for a best man, I would really be lost to choose from all my friends who could have been a best man. I don't know if that's good or bad. My wife says, "You're funny when it comes to your friends sometimes. You treat them all alike. You don't single anybody special."

I said, "Well, I have a friend Lou Shanahan who's a good friend of mine." His wife and my wife are close, and we go out to shows or dinner together. The four of us usually do it. But I try—I consider everybody my friend, like, you know, who I know. And like I say, it's just like, she says to me, "Who's your best friend?"

I don't know who I could say is my best friend. I have to give just a little edge to my friend Lou Shanahan. I would say he's my best friend. Of course we go to dinner and stuff like that. Not that we have that much in common. All right, we have that much in common when it comes to money. We don't care when we go out, spending money. When I say that, we don't worry about who's going to pick up the tab or anything like that, where another guy would say, "Gimme $2.50 for that, gimme a dollar thirty for that, "we don't go that way. If the bill is $20, it's $10 apiece, stuff like that—we split everything down the middle, we don't quibble about who pays for the cab fare home. If the cab's $3 and we both get out of the cab he doesn't say to me, "Gimme a dollar fifty." I don't, if I pay for it, I don't say, "Give me $1.50." We just get along like that, you know—where I've gone out with fellows who say, "Well, you owe me $1.60

for this, pinching the pennies right down. I'd have to say Lou Shanahan would be my best friend today.

Q: How did you meet him? How long have you known him? From where?

Santangelo: Well, I've known Louie since 1950. I met him through sports, playing hockey, and we played against each other, and then the team that I was playing with broke up and I ended up going to his team, and we got involved. I'm three years older than Lou. When I was out of the service, he was just going in, because he was caught in that Korean stuff, 1950. So he did two years in the Marine Corps, although he's married—even though I'm three years older than him, he's one year and a half married longer than I am, you know. But his wife is a wonderful person, really wonderful person. Lou has two children. His daughter is 18, the same as mine, and his son is 16, the same as mine.

Q: Hockey teams go by parishes also?

Santangelo: No, they weren't parish teams in them days. In them days they were neighborhood teams, block teams, like you played for—When I first started playing, I was from the 89th Street mob, which was called the Bruins in them days. Louis played with the Olympics which was from 93rd.

Q: Roller hockey?

Santangelo: This was all roller hockey. We used to play down in Carl Schurz Park, which is where the Mayor of New York—it's three blocks away from the Mayor's mansion. The Mayor lives at 88th, on the Drive. The field was 84th on the Drive. And Danny Hart was from say the Packers. That was from St. Joseph Parish. That was the closest parish there, if you want to break it up into parishes, like, you know. But there was no parish. It was blocks. So we just got this league together, and it was—the Park Department ran the league, more or less. They organized—well, we organized our own teams, to play in the Park Department league, They would say that we're having a league this year, and the age was unlimited in them days, and we would go. After the war it was very big. Hockey was very big in this area.

Q: You'd roller skate on what kind of a surface?

Santangelo: A flat top more or less, blacktop. Blacktop, yeah.

Q: With a hockey stick and puck?

Santangelo: With a hockey stick and a roll of tape, which we used as a puck, yeah. In fact, in 1950 a Donald Hegan and another fellow, I forget his name, tried to start a league of indoor hockey. We played in the old St. Nicholas arena. This was playing on a wooden floor now. He tried to make it something like the roller derby is today only in hockey. We had teams from the West Side participating. We played in Jamaica arena. We played in St. Nicholas arena. We couldn't get Madison Square Garden because we weren't big enough, but we played in the armories, and they charged admission to get in, but the admission fee went, in them days, it was just who you could bring to the game. Your neighborhood would come out—the guys who always came out—maybe you had 50 or 60 people would be for your team, and say from 89th Street, and if you were playing the guys from 93rd that night, they'd bring maybe 50 or 60 people, That would be 120 people. But there were always double headers, There were teams from the West Side. Now, I remember one night we played in St. Nicholas Arena, and it was on Channel 13, televised. They were trying to do all these promotion gimmicks, to get the game off the ground. We had uniforms that the league gave us, and they were regular hockey uniforms but we used to go under crazy names, like the Bronx Miners, the Texas Rangers, the Manhattan Top Hats, the New York Rockets. I can remember the names.

But something happened to me in 1950 which, like I say, is a bit to my neighborhood fame. I was a fairly decent hockey player in them days, and my coach came to me, Mike Higgins, and he says, "Tony, I'm going to have your picture on *TV Guide."*

"Aw," I said, "You're kidding."

He said, "No. I'm working on it."

Well, Mike was a little bit of an exaggerator, and I said, "OK, Mike." I went along with it. So the other star of one of the other teams, Danny Hart, he already was on radio, to build up the sport. He had a five-minute interview on radio, and everybody knew that Danny was on radio, and I said, to Mike, "Danny Hart's on radio. You're putting me on *TV Guide.* I gotta see that."

Well, would you believe, three weeks later, *TV Guide* came out, and sure enough, there I was on the cover, on the inside cover, not the outside cover, but the cover, inside cover of *TV Guide,* 1950, advertising Cranford Clothes, who was televising, who was the sponsor for the roller hockey, for the so-called pro Roller Hockey League. That was the name of it, I think. 1950, and I still have a couple of copies up at my house. My kids are always kidding me about it.

Q: That must have been a great thing to see.

Santangelo: Well, it was in them days. I remember my father—imagine my father, he went out and bought 20 copies. And my mother still has a couple of copies today. People today don't believe me when I say it, and I hate to show the picture because, you know, it's going back years, it's over, what, 1950, it's 26 years ago, no, 24 years ago.

Q: Why do you hate to show it?

Santangelo: Well, I tell you, I was wearing white skates. Girls wore white skates in those days. You know, if I had black skates on it would be a little different, you know. Yeah, that had a lot to do with it, why I don't want to show, believe it or not, because when you go roller skating the girl's got the white skates and the fellow's got the black skates.

Q: Then how did you happen to get white skates for the picture?

Santangelo: They didn't have my size that night.

Q: I see. That's a hard situation.

Santangelo: It was a big thing in my life. You know. I remember that well. And my son is playing ice hockey today. He plays for Cardinal Hayes. He plays for this New York Greater Hockey League today which is sponsored by the New York Rangers today. And he kids around about roller hockey. Everybody says you couldn't be as good as your old man; they kid him like that, and he takes a little offense at it. And I don't blame him because they're not giving the kid a fair shake by telling him that. Nothing worse than growing up in the shadow of somebody. But he's pretty good. He's high scorer for Cardinal Hayes right now, and he's in this Greater New York Hockey League, where he plays with fellows from Brooklyn, Long Island, Lower Manhattan. He's not doing too bad, like he has the seventh highest score. He's not built the way I was when I was a kid. He's taller, but he doesn't have the weight. He's going to be a tall kid. In fact, he's my size now and he's like 16 years old, but he's got more opportunities than we'll ever have, today—the kids today. I didn't even know how to stand on ice skates in them days.

Q: Yeah. OK, were there any—you mentioned your first girl. When you were sixteen, your first girl friend.

Santangelo: My first one. That's right, Helen.

Q: In those days—you went steady with her?

Santangelo: I went steady with her, let's see, about three years, three years.

Q: When you went steady in those days, did people go to bed together at that time, or no?

Santangelo: No. You were afraid to go to bed in them days. Just the usual petting.

Q: They didn't go to bed in those days.

Santangelo: I didn't know about going to bed till I got in the Army, to tell you the truth. 'Till I saw my first film by the Army. I was only 18 years old. Like I say, the kids today are much advanced. I never knew what that thing was for 'till I got in the Army. Then I saw films on VD. Then I realized.

Q: Guys didn't talk about it?

Santangelo: Not in my crowd. It's unbelievable. Today, you know—

Q: I don't know if it's unbelievable, I just—

Santangelo: Sex was a nothing in them days. I mean, it came out like if I was alone with her or something like that, we'd do the usual—the petting bit, you know, and all that. But as for going to bed—no way. No way. That only came into my mind after the war.

Q: Did you have other girl friends, too?

Santangelo: No, she was my only girl 'till I came back after the service. And when I came out after the service, she was more or less engaged at the time.

She had busted my heart. I guess I was on the rebound, and I met another girl; she used to come down to watch the hockey games. Her name was Barbara, and naturally, she made me forget all about the other one, and it was just a run-of-the-mill thing. But I wasn't a big fellow for girls. Like I went out with Barbara; I went out with Barbara for about two years. But I think Barbara left me because I didn't have a steady job. She wanted to get married and everything like that. She was more or less the settling down type. And I wasn't ready to settle down. I didn't have a steady job, first of all.

Q: How old were you at that time, again?

Santangelo: Now I'm 21, when I'm going with Barbara. Now I'm thinking about the bed stage. But it never came off with Barbara. Just the usual bit, you know. I think I was a little afraid. Today, I mean, there's nothing to be afraid of today. I mean it's too easy for the kids. Not that—Hey, if this is the bit, let them do their bit, I mean, you know. I know people that are living together today, to see if they're going to get married, people that I know. It's shocking some of the parents, but what are they going to do about it?

Q: How old are the kids?

Santangelo: Today?

Q: Yes, that are living together.

Santangelo: Oh, I know one that's 19. Sure. 19 years old. At 19 I didn't think of nothing. Jesus. Unbelievable in them days.

Q: Yes, it's different. Things have changed, I guess, quite a bit.

Santangelo: That way. Unless I was too much involved with the sports. Maybe some other guys, all they'd think about would be something like that, but—it never came across. I used to like to take a girl out to a movie or to a hockey game, and maybe stop and have a drink or something like that, you know.

Q: How old were you when you met your wife? Tell me how you met her and all that.

Santangelo: I had known my wife through a friend of mine, Frank. He had—this fellow I also played hockey with, he said, "Gee, there's a great gal that you would really hit it off with"; you're two great people and all that, you know, "You have a lot in common. She's my best friend, you're one of my best friends; I wish you'd get together."

I met her, "Hello, how are you," but nothing ever came out of it. And then one day I was playing stickball in the street and she was looking out the window. I said, "Hello, how are you," bing bing, she came down—

I played a lot of softball after I finished playing—my baseball days were over. I played softball with the neighborhood bar teams around here. We have our own league. And she came up. She was babysitting for her cousin one day. When the game was over, I was walking back and I just happened to be walking alongside her, "Hello, how are you." It was a warm day and I said, "Would you like to stop in for a Tom Collins? Have a drink?"

She said, "OK," so she stopped in, and that's how it started. We had a drink and I said, "How about a movie? How about a bar?" The next thing I knew, 27 years old, I was going down the aisle.

Q: How long did you go with her before you got married?

Santangelo: I went with her about a year. About a year, yeah.

Q: What do you think attracted you to her? As compared to other girls.

Santangelo: Just like my friends said. She was a very congenial person. Very congenial. She made everything easy for me, conversation-wise. She liked what I liked in life. We were very compatible more or less.

Q: What things did she like?

Santangelo: Well, the movies. She liked that. She loved sports. We used to do everything together like, you know. And there were the neighborhood rackets. It's a funny thing, but we even, when we dance, we just danced and I never stepped on her feet, like some girls could never follow me, and I guess that led to it too. Little things, you know. Just the little things that made life easier. It made me want to be with her, and her vice versa; you know what I mean.

Q: You like movies a lot.

Santangelo: Love movies. Love them.

Q: Did your brother like movies?

Santangelo: He used to go to movies a lot, but I think he got away from the movies more or less.

Q: Do you think it was as important to him as it was to you?

Santangelo: No. Never. No. I used to go like, when I was a kid, I used to go three times a week to the movies. I'd see chapters on Saturdays—Flash Gordon, Dick Tracy, you name them. My big idol when I was a kid was Johnny Weissmuller in Tarzan.

Q: Who did you go with ? Did you go alone usually, or—

Santangelo: When I was a kid I used to go with another schoolmate. We used to go together more or less and the two of us used to see everything that played up in the neighborhood, you know. Then I saw an awful lot with my mother, like I said, with the passes that she had. I never got away from the movies.

Q: How did she get those passes?

Santangelo: Well, a friend of my father's used to come into the place, and he used to drink in the place. He was the captain of the ushers up in the theatre, and in them days they used to put signs in the bars telling you what was playing, so if they put that sign in, they had to give you a pass. My father used to get the passes from him.

Q: He'd never go and you would take your mother. You were what, a teen-ager then?

Santangelo: Oh, before I was a teenager, three, four, yeah, gee. A long time, I've been going to the movies.

Q: With your mother—

Santangelo: Great.

Q: OK. You mentioned I guess the people who were most important to you. Think back. What would you say were the major decisions you had to make in your life, including not just as a grownup but as a kid?

Santangelo: I think my first probably major decision was quitting school. I knew I didn't like it. I knew I wasn't getting anyplace by it. I was only wasting time, you know, more or less to speak. I went a half a year supposedly to school and I never went there. I was getting all the cards that the school was sending and playing like what is known as hookey. I used to go down to the Paramount and see Frank Sinatra in them days and all, you know, save my money that my mother would give me for carfare to go to a show. But I guess, this decision then was to quit school. That was one of my big ones.

Q: Other friends didn't quit at the same time or anything, just you?

Santangelo: Just me by myself. I was hanging out with people who didn't go to school then too. More or less were just hanging around and working. And that could have been a little bit of an influence on it. But my mind wasn't on it. So I said to myself, "You aren't getting anyplace, and you're only going to be trouble and left back and stay after school and all that, so let's just go home and—."I got caught playing hookey. My father came in. I'll tell you, it broke my father's heart more than my mother's heart. And he said to me, "What have you been doing? You didn't go to school for six months ?" I said, "That's right. I'm sorry but I just don't—."

"Well, you gotta; don't you want to go back?"

I said, "No. I don't want to go back. I want to work." And I didn't realize it at that time, but I made a decision that I'd be working the rest of my life. He said, he told me, "You're going to work the rest of your life, if you don't go back to that school, because you're going to have to need money, you're going to have to bring money into the house, you've gotta give your mother money" and blah blah blah. That's just the way it went on. So I consider that a big decision in my life. Yeah. What else? School . . .

I guess getting married was the next big one. Getting married. You know, giving up your single life and everything like that.

Q: Did you find that hard to do? Do you think you didn't really want to get married?

Santangelo: My wife claims I never gave it up. Oh, all my friends had got-ten married. You know. They were getting married. Like I say, we would fall one at a time, it seemed like. 1954 was the year that there were eight marriages out of my crowd. I mean, starting with January right to December, like, Danny Hart, my friend who played hockey, I mentioned him before, he got married the end of January. Howie Foster got married that year. Valentine's Day, he got married. Rudy Bauer got married Washington's Birthday. I ended up getting married in August that year. There was two marriages after me, there was probably two more in front of me, but seven or eight of us got wiped out that year. So the whole crowd went together. We were all going, you know, for a few years with our so-called wives now that they are. So I guess that was a big decision.

Q: Your wife thinks you still live like a single man in some ways?

Santangelo: Well, yeah. Like I can be walking down the street, and, say, I have to be home for dinner at 5 and I can be walking down the street and meet somebody like I haven't seen like in 12 years, and we could talk, maybe stop and have a drink, and I'll call her. She'll understand me. She'll say, "I never seen a guy meet so many people like you can meet," you know. "You've always got an excuse for something," you know.

I'm not going to say she's wrong. She's probably right. Now that I'm in this building line, I find myself stopping after work, you know, having a drink or two with the fellows, getting involved playing the machine. Sometimes supper's at 6, I walk in at 8. With a few drinks under my belt. But I'm very mellow. I'm happy. She's a little annoyed. But she accepts it. She more or less goes along with everything. But it's a different game now. I mean I'm in the building line. Sometimes you have to stop and have a drink, you know, more or less to keep your contacts going, to get the jobs. That's the way it goes today, you know.

Q: You're on different jobs, so a foreman who's looking for workers—is that how it goes?

Santangelo: Well, you get your job out of the union, you know. Out of the hall. You go to your job. And naturally you meet somebody, you know, and you work with him, so say it's a holiday, like Christmas, "let's stop and have a drink. " It's just goodwill, you know, that's all it is. It's not that you're going to end up becoming an alcoholic or anything like that. You just get closer to the guy. The job ends maybe in four months and you're off to another job.

Q: You don't see the guy again?

Santangelo: You might run across him. You might run across him maybe two years later. Who knows ? You know, that's the way it is. It's like being in the Army. You meet so many good people. And you meet bad people too, you know, but nine out of ten are real good fellows, in the building line, the hard hats, we call them.

Q: Do you wear a hard hat?

Santangelo: Yes, I do. I wear a hard hat.

Q: You mentioned before something about Department of Sanitation. Was that your father's idea that you should go to work there or what?

Santangelo: That was my father's idea, yes.

Q: How old were you at that time?

Santangelo: I was 19. Just got out, just got outa the service.

Q: Back from the service—you quit school, you worked in construction or—

Santangelo: For a year I didn't do a thing.

Q: Didn't do a thing; that took you to 17 and a half roughly.

Santangelo: Right.

Q: You quit at 16 and a half?

Santangelo: Yeah, and then I went to work delivering orders. I delivered orders, yeah, like I was working full time. I was a delivery boy. For a grocery store.

Q: Right, and then you worked for a while—

Santangelo: Just before I went into the Army, I was working for United Railway Express, REA. On a shipping dock. I worked there six months. Loading trucks. Then I went in the Army. I come out of the Army. I did nothing for a year. Then I went to work for Coca-Cola for eight months, on the platform, loading and unloading, yeah, production, they call it. Then from there, I got laid off in the winter months because it was a seasonal job, and then that's when my father says, "You gotta get your fanny going" so, that's when he got me the connection in the building line. I went to work in construction.

Q: It was at the same time he thought maybe you ought to look into Department of Sanitation?

Santangelo: He told me that I was foolish, because in them days, the taverns always had their political leaders in the area and everything like that, and there was jobs available, and they said, my father said to me, "You can go onto the Department of Sanitation, no testing required." This was 1947, late '47, he offered me this job. He said, "You can go on, take it. Kid, take it, don't be a fool."

Q: Your father got someone to offer it to you.

Santangelo: Someone said to my father, "Do you know anybody wants to go on the DS? No test involved, nothing involved, we can get him on." You know what I mean?

So I says, "Great, but not for me. It's 5 and a half days, I don't want to work 5 and a half days." And yet, later on in life, I worked in the restaurant six days a week for 16 years. So you know how it works out. You get involved in a business—and I wasn't a partner or nothing, just a man on salary.

Q: Do you think you made a wrong decision not to go in the DS?

Santangelo: I ask myself that question so many times it's not funny. In a way I regret it, not being able to say, I could be retired now. But for all that's happened to me through the years, meeting the different classes of people in the bar business, the numerous friends I've made in construction, I don't regret it at all, no.

Q: What periods of your life do you like to look back on?

Santangelo: I guess I like to look back on that period when I was single and playing sports mostly. Like the period right after the war, I would say. Like not being able to work and just walk around with money in your pocket was great, lounging around. We used to call ourselves "beach bums" in them days. Used to always go to Rockaway and lay on the beach. We used to pool our money. It was, what you had, I had. We all were guys—there was three or four with me that didn't work for a year, so I wasn't alone. We made $20 a week.

Q: Unemployment compensation?

Santangelo: It was unemployment from the government. Yeah. And we got that check every week. And if I went to the beach and had $3, and you had $2.50 or you had a dollar, the guy who had the dollar had just as much as we did because we all pooled our money. We all ate hot dogs. We always had our carfare. And we always—it was different. We had a real close relationship. These were the fellows from St. Ignatius I'm talking about, by the way. But they all went on to take aptitude tests for jobs. I didn't. I didn't take the aptitudes. They were giving aptitude tests then.

Q: These were city jobs mostly—fire, police?

Santangelo: No, them fellows—to see what you were suitable for, like the insurance man and everything like that.

Q: Who gave them those aptitude tests?

Santangelo: They were giving them down at the Cathedral, down at St. Patrick's, down around there someplace.

Q: Who sponsored it?

Santangelo: I have no idea. I just remembered. The word aptitude stuck with me and I just remembered it and I thought I'd let it out right now.

Q: How come you didn't go down there yourself?

Santangelo: I never figured I was a smart kid. I knew these kids were always smarter than me, from St. Ignatius. Maybe it was the education they had. I don't know. They took time out. I didn't really take time out. I wasn't much for opening a book after I got out of grammar school.

Q: Most of them finished high school?

Santangelo: They all did. All did. Everyone of that crowd finished.

Q: I see. That didn't bother you. They didn't consider it because the main thing was the sports. You were good at it—

Santangelo: That was acceptable to them.

Q: So it didn't matter. You didn't ever think about it?

Santangelo: Well, I'll tell you, I used to think about it a lot, you know, be-cause they were graduates from St. Anne's, from Regis, which is one of your top schools in the city, I think, today even, which is strictly a scholarship school, and three of them went on to graduate from Fordham, two went on to St. John's—colleges even, you know what I mean? Then there was a few that just did their high school and just dropped out. But they never made fun of me, anything like that, you know, education-wise, no.

Q: So you think this period right after the war was the best period of your life.

Santangelo: I'd say undoubtedly the best period of my life.

Q: When you weren't working—one year that you weren't working.

Santangelo: That was a fabulous year for me. Really fabulous year. Playing ball. Not working. Everything like that, you know. I just was in like a rut, but it was a good rut, a happy rut. I wasn't alone. I had a lot of friends with me, eve-rything like that. We all did the same bit.

Q: Then why did it end?

Santangelo: It didn't end. It ended. I had to go to work, more or less; that ended it. I ran out of cash and then I had to go to work. But I was very happy then, too.

Q: That changed your life then.

Santangelo: Well, it started changing my thinking a little bit, you know.

Q: What periods of your life would you rather not think about?

Santangelo: Yeah. . . . I don't like to think about the nights that my father came home drunk and arguing over petty things with my mother when I was laying in bed. Things like that. Those are the only really bad things that bother me. I believe like, if you're going to argue in front of kids, try not to argue in front of kids, you know. It's tough sometimes. To argue in front of kids, I believe it leaves every kid scarred. I believe I was scarred with the arguments of my mother and father. Like my wife loved my father, and loves my mother, you know, but sometimes women don't always agree, you know—But she didn't know my father the way I knew him. I lived with him. She lived on vaca-tions—you know, we used to spend a couple of days with him when he took his vacation, everything like that. She seen a little bit of him. My father idol-ized my wife. He really loved her. And vice versa. My wife thought the world of him. But she didn't see him like I seen him. And these are the things I like to put out of my mind, like. You know what I mean, things like that. And then also, like when my daughter was first born, she had a, contracted a—I don't know, a germ called roseola, medical term for, you run a very high fever and we thought we were going to lose her. Something like that.

Q: What effect do you think your father's quarreling with your mother had on you? What do you think it did to you?

Santangelo: It made me feel sorry for my mother. Every time I heard it. I didn't like my father for it, you know. I didn't like him at all for it, even though I knew I was his—but I still was afraid of him, you gotta remember that, like I mentioned, and I didn't like stand up to my father till I came out of the service. I used to tell him, "Why don't you stop?" and all this if he acted up. I would say, "Why don't you stop it now?" You know. Not—I respected him. He would tell me to shut up, mind your own business. I'd say "All right, but give us a break, give the neighbors a break." You know, stuff like that.

I never appreciated those arguments, because they used to happen at 3:30, 4 o'clock in the morning, when he'd come home, and I'd be trying to get up for school and I'd listen. I'd lay in bed, and his language was pretty bad too, you know what I mean, and I couldn't see that. I couldn't believe that was my father. I couldn't believe that.

Then I got to know why later on in years, you know, like—not why he was arguing, but that was his way of speaking. You know what I mean? He had a way of calling you an SOB which sounded like honey. You wouldn't think nothing of it. Where you could say it to another guy, he'd want to fight you. But Father had a gift about him, like how to speak to people. It's unbelievable. Well, he met all walks of life in there. I'll tell you, if you ever want to go into a business to meet all types of people, just go into the bar business.

Q: That's really where you meet them.

Santangelo: Because when people drink, you see so many sides of people. You see their so-called good side, and you see their bad side. It comes right out, right in front of you. You would never believe what you see in people. And I've seen it happen to so many people, it's unbelievable. You get some education in a bar. You know. I got some experience. That's why you said, would you like to live—I don't think so. I think I learned an awful lot about people. And how to handle people. You know, stuff like that. How to cope with them. Their troubles. Like you become a priest when you're a bartender, you become a father, to the younger people. You listen to everybody's troubles. It's a known fact that a bartender just has an ear for troubles. The idea is to keep your mouth shut when you're a bartender. That's the idea. Not to pass it on, not pass it on. Just accept it, keep it inside you, and don't let on what's going on. That's what I believe. And I heard so many stories that my hair curls sometimes. People in the neighborhood, you know. Wives and husbands, unbelievable.

Q: You heard a lot.

Santangelo: Oh, yeah. It's funny. I'd come home and my wife would say, "Did you hear about so and so?" and I already knew this story a month ago. And I'd say, "No." She'd say, "You hadda hear it." I'd say, "Well, yeah." "How come you don't tell me?" I'd say, "Well, it's none of my business, I don't wanta—" "But you heard it, why didn't you tell me?" I'd say, "Why should you know it? You feel better that you know it?" You know, stuff like that.

She'd say, "Well, why should I hear it second hand all the time?"

I don't say nothing. Even though I'm not in the bar business anymore, I found out what they don't know don't hurt them. It's an old expression, but I believe in not saying a word.

Q: That leads up to another kind of question. Maybe you've thought about it. What kind of a person would you say you are?

Santangelo: Well, I'd better give you my opinion, not my wife's.

Q: That's right. You can tell me your wife's later, but I want yours, how you think of yourself, see yourself, right.

Santangelo: How I see myself is, I feel I'm a very compatible person. I think I'm very easy to get along with. I talk mostly, I can talk mostly anything with people. I try to keep up on current events and stuff like that. I'm in a new field now of work that I haven't been in like in 17 years, and I make friends very easily. I think I'm a selfish person at times. Not that I deprive anybody from anything, but I always take care of myself and see that I have the best. If I'm out with my friends, I mean, I want everything to be right down the middle. I don't like to see anybody get hurt, like when I say hurt, like we're not rich in this neighborhood. You know how we live. I don't believe somebody should spend $5 more than I did, and I don't believe I should spend $5 more than the other guy did. That's about it. I don't know what else I could say in that respect, how I am. You ask the questions.

Q: Right, that's OK. I'll ask questions, you answer whatever comes to mind, then I'll ask more questions. I'd like to follow up with, how do you think you came to be the kind of person you are? You've described yourself in a certain way.

Santangelo: Well, I'll tell you, that's a good question. I think those fellows from St. Ignatius had an awful lot to do with my life. I had met fellows like—I was growing up with guys you know like I told you, one was a fighter, one held up a gas station, and everything like that, you know. Then when this Charlie Rooney took me over to Ignatius, I met a whole different crowd.

Q: Were you 19 at that time?

Santangelo: No, this was just before I went in the service.

Q: So you were about 17.

Santangelo: Right, 17 I met them. Then I went away. Then when I came back I went right back there. And I think around 17, that age more or less really, being around these fellows—I believe it's who you grow up with, more or less. They didn't do anything out of the ordinary, but just the way they conducted themselves. Never out of hand. Used to go up to the poolroom and shoot a game of pool, nothing like that, never anything mischievous like the other crowd did, you know what I mean? Like I told you, like before 17, the guys would like steal this and steal that and steal the paper; they'd steal anything, you know what I mean? I'm not saying these other fellows were better off. Maybe their fathers had better jobs than—and they could afford to send them to St. Ignatius. But they lived in the parish, so if you lived in the parish it didn't cost you any money to go to school. But it was just the way they accepted one another over there. And they pulled for each other. They pulled for each other, you know what I mean?

Q: You hadn't had that in the earlier group.

Santangelo: No. It was an individualist group in them days. They were individualists.

Q: How do you think you managed to avoid—you went with those guys for most of your life, till 17, how did you manage not to—not to do some of the same things the other kids did? I gather you were in that group, yet you didn't go in for the stealing they did. I guess they were getting into trouble before they were 17 and you didn't.

Santangelo: Right.

Q: How do you think you managed that?

Santangelo: Well, here's what happened. After the war—before the war, I started to play ball with these fellows from St. Ignatius. And I would play ball for St. Ignatius, but I was still hanging out with my old friends. Now, I was like between the two groups. The group that I used to hang out with, you know, that I was brought up with, wasn't that much interested in sports. I found out that I had to go out of the neighborhood more or less to get into organized sports. They would play, but they would play if they had nothing to do, more or less, you know what I mean? Well, I always wanted to play. So when I got involved with this St. Ignatius group, they were more like, you know, sports-minded, and everything was sports, sports. I found myself more or less doing that.

Then I went into the service. When I came back out of the service, there were still the two groups but like I say, the group that I was brought up with in the early part of my life was older than me. They were more advanced than me. Now they are in the bars. It's after the war now. They're drinking in bars. This is the big thing, after the war.

All right, I'm 20 years old, right? They're in the bars, and my friends from St. Ignatius are on the ball field. On Saturdays they're playing ball. My friends around here are in bars, they're drinking in the afternoon, maybe they're playing a game of stickball you know or something like that, they're playing for a bottle of beer, while I'm playing for the love of the game. I'm playing with guys who want to play the game.

I believe that that was the turning point of what turned me around, more or less, these fellows from St. Ignatius, that group there.

Q: But before you ever knew St. Ignatius, when you were younger, you didn't get into the same kind of mischief that the other guys did.

Santangelo: Maybe I was chicken. Maybe I was scared.

Q: You think so?

Santangelo: I think I was scared of my father an awful—I had a great fear of my father, like I say, that my mother had put in me. She'd say, "Don't be bad, I'll tell your father, don't do this, I'll tell your father," you know. It could have been that. But I never did things like that when I was a kid. I believed that stealing was wrong. Yet I did it myself, later on, you know. But like I say, I never held up a bank. I would like take an apple off the stand or a piece of candy from a counter.

Q: But I gather these other kids were doing more than that by the time they were 16, 17. Their activities had gone past that point already, didn't they?

Santangelo: Oh yeah. Well, see, I got caught stealing a box of toothpicks in the A & P.

Q: How old were you then?

Santangelo: About 14. And I never forgot it. The manager scared the living daylights out of me.

Q: What did he say?

Santangelo: He said, "I'm gonna take you home. I'm gonna do this, gonna do that." I said, "Gee, I'll never do it again. I'm sorry" you know. And the funny thing about this, I had 12 cents in my pocket and the toothpicks cost six cents at the time. He said, "You're gonna pay for these toothpicks" and I said, "Yeah, I'll pay for them." So I paid the six cents and he threw me out of the store. I walked home. I had a thousand toothpicks in my pocket that I didn't need. And it wasn't the idea, it was just to go along with the other guys, to show that I'd like to be one of them, take something, I guess, that's what it was, they were taking this—and so I grabbed a box of toothpicks. Never forget that. Scared the hell out of me.

Q: That's interesting, to hear that. So you think that really helped keep you on a different path?

Santangelo: Oh yes. Definitely.

Q: You mentioned before, what does your wife think of you? What's her view of you?

Santangelo: I'm a spoiled brat. I get everything I want. I do anything I want to do.

Q: Would she like to change you, you think?

Santangelo: Oh, I think she'd like to see me more attentive to her, like take her out more often, everything like that, you know. We go out, but it's probably too far apart like, you know what I mean? But with the change of jobs and everything, I find myself stopping off with the fellows now and talking, everything like that, and she probably wants—she's staying right on my back. I hope she doesn't think I'm going to turn out like my father, like, you know—

One thing about drinking, I can drink, and if I've had this said to me once, I've had it said to me 20 times. They say to me, "Tony, I don't know how you can drink, were you a bartender? You didn't drink behind the bar. You used to come up from behind the bar and start drinking. You could drink for three hours, you could drink for six hours, your disposition never changed, you could see that you were getting to feel good—but you never got drunk, you never fell, never got sloppy, you never got abusive, you'd just pick yourself up and go home."

I said, "Yeah, I do that because when I get a certain amount of drink in me, I get sick. I'm like a tank. I know if I take that one more drink, I'm gonna throw up and vomit and it's gonna ruin me, and I don't do that. I just stop."

Even today I'll do that. I will stop. I will get to a certain point and stop. If I'm having a good time and there's a full drink there, I'll just leave it there, and I'll sip it—maybe I don't wanta go home because everybody's there, we're playing the machine for a quarter a game, you know, pastime, and guys will drink and crack cars up. I have a friend that he wrecks a car a year. I say, "You're lucky." Stitches in his face, all over his body. I say, "Danny, you're the luckiest guy in the world. You walk away from these things."

He says, "Tony, I don't know what it is. I get behind that wheel, I wanta go home." He owns his own home up in New City. He says, "I gotta drive home."

I say, "Why don't you stay in the city or stop drinking?"

He says, "Yeah, everybody ain't like you. You just stop. You just stop. I don't know how you do it."

I said, "I don't know if it's will power or not, but I wouldn't care if I had—a drink puts me in a nice frame of mind. You know, I believe if you're cranky, if you have a few drinks, you know, sometimes it changes your attitude."

I never drink when I'm working, because it's too dangerous, my job. I'll drink after work. I'll stop and I'll drink every day. I can have three or four, ten or eleven. It doesn't change my disposition. But some fellows, what it does to them, it's unbelievable.

Q: You can have 10, 11 drinks, it doesn't change your disposition?

Santangelo: Doesn't bother me at all.

Q: What are you drinking, mixed drinks?

Santangelo: Well, I drink rye and water, I drink VO and water.

Q: You can drink 10 or 11 of those.

Santangelo: It won't bother me. When I say my disposition, I mean, I'll start to maybe feel it and I'll say, "It's time to go," and I'll go home, and I'll come home, I'll be starved, supper will be over and I'll say, "I know, don't start, just tell me where it is, I'll take a TV dinner." I just don't want to hear nothing. "How come you stay with your friends, you can't stay with your family?" You know, little bits. That's not right. Just get involved. I happen to be a fellow who can get involved very easy. Very easy. I'm very easily like get involved. If you start talking something, I can get in the conversation—talk, talk, drink, drink. But I will never deprive my family out of any money or anything like that.

Q: I see. You don't have any money hassles with your wife?

Santangelo: I have plenty of money hassles with my wife, but it'll never be over drinking. You know what I mean? I believe like if I work in six degree weather, like I did a couple of weeks ago, I believe I'm entitled. Maybe here's where the selfish part comes in. I believe I'm entitled to stop, if there's a couple of guys. "What kind of a day was it, was it cold where you were working?" and before you know it, we're—I believe this is—

She believes, "Why don't you come home, get a hot cup of soup, take a hot shower, get under the covers, relax?" You know.

I would never spend any money drinking that would deprive my kids from anything. Shoes on their feet or anything like that, food on the table. No way. Like I already said to myself, I think I'm drinking a little too much now. I'm not going to drink Monday, Tuesday, or Wednesday. Thursday, everybody gets paid, and Friday—so Thursday and Friday, Saturday, Sunday, it don't bother me about the weekend drinking, but I mean just Thursday and Friday, everybody gets together. In this neighborhood it's a way of life. Not that you drink, it's just the companionship you get there, you see your friends.

Q: You go to the same place all the time?

Santangelo: Same place, yes. Joe Wagner's up here on Second Avenue. We go up there and we all meet. Joe's a very good personal friend of mine. I played ball for him. I played ball for him for 20 years. That's my hangout.

Q: Let's see, OK. I asked you what kind of person you are and how you came to be that kind of person. Let's ask you now to look at how you've changed in the course of your life. In other words, what are the most important changes and what caused the changes in you? How did they happen? You probably haven't thought about it in this way, but maybe think about that.

Santangelo: Experience. Getting older.

Q: More specifically, what are the changes? In what ways actually, have you, Tony Santangelo, changed?

Santangelo: Have I changed?

Q: Yes, from the way you were at one time of life to the way you were at another time of life.

Santangelo: I don't know how to explain that. I'm really at a loss for words at this question here. For me being changed. Have I gone through a big change in life?

Q: At any time. Do you think you're the same kind of person—

Santangelo: All through life?

Q: Yeah.

Santangelo: I don't think I've changed hardly at all. People tell me I haven't changed, even in appearance. Here when they haven't seen me in years. No, I don't think I've changed at all. I thought maybe you meant in the way of experience, wiser, something like that, you know what I mean?

Q: I mean more in the kind of person you are. It might not be a total change, that you'd be unrecognizable from one time to another. People don't usually change so completely, but often they feel they've changed in a certain way.

Santangelo: I don't know. As I say, I think I've gotten mellower, but I don't see how, I mean,—I really can't say. I don't really think I have.

Q: Well, let's turn it around. In what ways have you stayed the same?

Santangelo: Well, I don't think my attitude has changed for meeting people. I accept people for what they are, you know. I don't judge anybody; if I like them I like them. There's all types of people in this world. You're always meeting somebody. Like I'm always meeting somebody new. I was always meeting somebody new in the bar business. I'm always meeting somebody new in this construction business, you know, and I take people for what, how they come across to me. I mean, like I say, there's not many people in this world that I don't get along with. In fact, I don't know who I don't get along with. Like if you say to me "Tony, do you have an enemy?" I'd say, "I really can't say that I do. If I do, I don't know him."

Q: You never had an enemy in your life. Even as a kid? Did you have enemies when you were a kid?

Santangelo: Nope, the only enemies I had were in competition in sports, I think—who was better than who. That would be the only clash I've had of personalities. I can remember, like you say, "This guy's better than you." I say, "Well, if he's better than me, he's gotta score more than me," you know. It would be like we were going for the scoring title or something like that. A guy I didn't even know him, only from playing against him. But like I can walk in anywhere, everybody says hello to Tony. I'm not saying that I'm a saint, I mean, you know—I believe they like me, unless they have something against me. I've never seen anybody walk down to the other end of the bar, or cross the street when I'm coming down the path, to say hello to me. I'll put it to you that way.

Q: You don't feel somebody's your enemy and you either have to watch out for him or—

Santangelo: No. Never felt that way. Never felt that way.

Q: Let's see, shall we go another half an hour? It's 4:30.

Santangelo: 4:30? It's 4:30 now?

Q: Yeah, you didn't believe it?

Santangelo: I didn't believe it at all.

Q: See, I told you, time goes faster than you think. You want to quit now, or go for another half hour?

Santangelo: Shall we go to 5?

Q: It's fine with me if it's OK with you.

Santangelo: Sure, let's keep going.

Q: All right, let's go to 5. I'd like you to think of some times when someone has tried to persuade you to do something, and they were not successful, that is, you didn't want to do what they wanted. Think of times like that, episodes in your life, when someone wanted to persuade you to do something. I'd like you to recall that in as much—think of times like that.

Santangelo: To go someplace or do something?

Q: Whatever. They wanted to persuade you.

Santangelo: Well, I've often turned people down for wanting to do something that I didn't want to do. Know what I mean, like they want to go here, they want to go there, and I say, "I don't want to go."

Q: Like where?

Santangelo: Like even today, they might say, "Let's go down to the West Side to this bar down there." Now, I happen to know it's a pretty rough place, you know, and they'll say, "Come on, let's go down and we'll see so and so." I'll say, "I don't want to go." You know. "Oh, come on, come on, we'll have a few drinks down there," something like that, and I'll say, "No, I don't want to go," and I don't go.

Q: Why do they want to go? They want to see someone there that they know?

Santangelo: They want to go down there and see somebody, but I know it's a rough neighborhood, and I don't think we need that. We're in our own neighborhood now, and I don't see why we should make that trip, first of all go crosstown and go all the way down to around 19th Street and Tenth Avenue to see people.

Q: Is it someone you know too, if they say, "Let's go see so and so?"

Santangelo: Well, they know him a little better than I do. It's really not that much interesting for me to go down, you know, and I can't see doing something like that, you know what I'm talking about?

Q: Yeah. And it doesn't bother them that it's a rough neighborhood?

Santangelo: No, they don't care. Some of these construction fellows don't care what they get into, you know.

Q: And you can see there could be trouble.

Santangelo: It could develop into trouble. You're going outa your neighborhood, you're going into a tough section of New York, and some of the fellows are touchy when they drink, some of the fellows I drink with are touchy. I know how to handle them, you know, if they get touchy, and if I see that they're getting an attitude about them, I just say, "Well, I'll see you tomorrow."

And I just pick myself up and leave. I don't know if it's been passed down, or it's a sixth sense or whatever you want to call it. I just feel like, if there's trouble brewing, I don't want no part of it. Unless it breaks. I mean, if two of my friends break out into an argument or fight, I'll be the first one to break it up and say, "Why don't you act your age?" or something like that. I can't—one thing that really bothers me is seeing two friends fight each other. It really bothers me. And I've seen it, and it just bothers me, and I let them know about it too. Like I mean, we're grown up now and I say, "Jesus, there are so many people in the world you could fight with, how can you fight with somebody that's your friend for 20 years" or something like that? But I've seen it through the years. I've seen it through the years, and drink has an awful lot to do with it. Drinking has an awful lot to do with trouble.

Q: OK, that's one kind of thing that happens every once in a while.

Santangelo: Oh, that happens quite often. Let's go here, let's go there, you know.

Q: Are there other people who try to persuade you to do things? That sometimes you don't want to do.

Santangelo: Well, they want you to go places with them. Nine out of ten, they want you to go to the track sometimes, you know, gambling, go to the races. "Let's go to the races." I could have maybe $30, $40 on me, you know, and I'd say, "No, I'm not that much of a gambler." I don't mind going to the track occasionally, you know. When I say occasionally, I mean once a year. If I go once a year, it's enough for me. I'm happy. But they'll say, "Come on, we'll take Frankie's car and we'll go up to the track." I'll say I don't want to go. "Aw, come on, don't be like that," they'll say.

I don't want to go. I can't see—maybe I got the money to go, maybe I'd rather do something better with my money at that time—just stay there, just go home and have that much tomorrow, then go up and take a chance, if I'm in the mood to go. I'm the type, if I want to go to the track, I'll say, "Let's pick a date. Maybe next Tuesday we'll all go to the track." I'd rather organize something than just straggle along and say, "Let's go here." You know what I mean; maybe I'm not in the mood to go. I hate to say I'm a moody person, but there's times when they say, "Let's go—"

I'll put it this way, if it's convenient for me, like I tell you, here's that selfish part I believe in me coming out again—if it's convenient for me, I'll do it. It's not convenient for me, I won't go out of my way to do It. I've already went out of my way to do things with people, you know, and done it, just because I don't want to hear anything. I'm sick and tired of hearing I don't go anyplace. If it's convenient for me, I'll do it.

Like I remember, about a year ago they said, "Let's go to Hoboken for clams." It was a Saturday afternoon. I said, "All the way to Hoboken for clams? Gee whiz." "Come on, let's go," and it was like 1 o'clock in the afternoon on a Saturday. So I ended up going to Hoboken for clams. I don't like clams, and I end up going out there for clams. They ate clams, blah blah blah, they ate this, they ate that. I had a roast beef sandwich. It was horrible. I didn't get home till 6:30 at night. My wife said, "Where were you?"

I said, "I was in Hoboken." "What were you doing in Hoboken?" I said, "Well, they said we were going to go to Hoboken, I just let me go, you know." She says, "So you went to Hoboken. Did you have a good time?"

I said, "I had a miserable time. "But maybe it's the frame of mind I was going to Hoboken, too, you know. I didn't want to go in the first place, but I end up going. When I do something like that, like they could say to me, "Let's go to Hoboken" and a year from now I'll say, "No thank you, I won't go to Hoboken."

But something like that, you know, where I go and I don't have a good time—it bothers me, you know.

Q: Why do you think you went that time?

Santangelo: I think I went because more or less they were breaking my back, you know. Well, I used to, I haven't been out there in about seven years. I went for two reasons, one because I was really curious to see what it looked like, if it's changed and all, which it had changed. They let the girls at the bar out here. It's the Clam House. They never let women at the bar out here—in Hoboken, in this Clam House. Women years ago never were allowed at the bar. They were allowed at the tables. Now, they're allowed at the bar. Not that we went with women. The wives didn't go. We were just drinking—we had moved a friend of ours that day in the morning, and we went back to Wagner's to where we meet: we were having a few drinks and some of the fellows said, "Let's take a ride to Hoboken."

So I said, "I'm not a big fish eater. I'm not a clam eater." But the curiosity of not being out there in a few years bothered me, and then I just didn't want to listen to them with all their abuse that I would have to listen to if I didn't go. So this is why I went, you know.

Q: These are not the same guys?

Santangelo: No, these are neighborhood fellows that I hang out with now.

Q: So they aren't construction workers.

Santangelo: They are construction workers in another field. I don't work with them. We all work in construction, mostly, but they're all different fields of it, different trades. Steamfitters, wirelappers, plumbers, ironworkers, tinsmiths, carpenters. They're all different trades.

Q: I'm interested in the fact that these guys did persuade you to go to Hoboken, but the other guys who wanted you to go down to Tenth Avenue didn't succeed in persuading you. Now, wouldn't they be abusive too or something like that? What's the difference?

Santangelo: Yeah. Let them talk. No, they would just get it off their chests. Like they're in there drinking, they had like a half a load on, they would just say, "Aw, you stiff" or something like that. Then it might have been the time of day they were going. They were going down there at night; like we were going in the afternoon to Hoboken. I would never go to Hoboken at night. Forget about it. Hoboken happened to be in the afternoon, at 2 o'clock in the afternoon. That's why I went out there. The time of day had a big thing to do with that.

Q: How about the difference in the two groups. Would that have anything to do with it?

Santangelo: Same people, more or less. Same people. Oh yes. Two of them were the same group.

Q: I see. Not different people, just the occasion.

Santangelo: I think it's what offers me. I hate to bring that selfish part back in there, but I think it's what I know, down there, you know. Like if they want to go someplace where I haven't seen somebody in a while, I'll go. I don't believe everybody should come to me, because when I was in the business I knew everybody had to come to me, because I served liquor and they used to come. See, my friends used to come and see me. Now it's the other way around. Some fellows from the West Side, they don't see me. So I know they're in a bar; it's for me to go see them now. And I make these trips occasionally. But there's times when I don't want to go. I'm just not going to go. And it depends on the money I have in my pocket at the time, too, whether I can afford it—I'm not going to tell them. I don't believe in letting anybody know what I got in my pocket. Like I could be walking around the street with a tuxedo on and have two cents in my pocket. You aren't going to think that when you see me. But I believe you shouldn't tell anybody what you have, and just give them some sort of excuse, pass it off.

Q: Think back. When you look back over your life and think of some of the difficult times you had, some of the problems, how did you get through those times, and what effect do you think all that had on you? Start with the earliest one you can remember.

Santangelo: Difficult times.

Q: Yes. What hard times did you have as a kid? Start with those.

Santangelo: Difficult times as a kid—well, the only thing I can think about difficult, about growing up, is I wasn't much of a fighter. I never got into many fights. I guess you'd call me a loser. But I didn't believe in fighting, you know. That didn't make you any better than the other fellow, I thought. But like I say, in those early days, like, that was a way of, not existing, not in the days of the Romans I mean, but neighborhood stuff was, you had to be tough, you know. And I just wasn't tough. But there was always like the guy who would always put the bull on you, you know, bully you, that's what I mean by that, like would push you around and say, you know, "You're nothing but a Mary" or something like that, "all you want to do is do this and do that." So I used to try to stay away from these guys, you know, these people. I knew, like I say, all these fellows are older than me. I grew up with fellows who were two or three years older than me, so if I was like nine, they were 12, you know, and if I was 12, they were 15, see, and the age gap there was big. And they always had that on me, you know.

Q: Did they take It out on you?

Santangelo: Well, it worked in both ways, too. I became like mascot of the crowd because I was the youngest; like nobody could touch me, you know what I mean, from another crowd, "Leave Tony alone."

Q: They'd stand up for you.

Santangelo: Oh, they would stick up for me on anything like that, you know, and I was always included in anything they did. I was like a little pet to have around sometimes. Although the only thing that really made me acceptable was the idea of playing sports. I was very good, even as a kid. I was better than some of the older fellows, you know. But when it came to fighting or anything like that, I wouldn't do it. I wouldn't fight anybody. They could push me around. In them days it was hitting you on the arm. They wouldn't hit you to hurt, or something like that—give you a shot in the arm or something. But some of the other fellows would step in and say, "Leave him alone," you know, "Do it with me " or something like that. "He's younger than you." "What do you mean he's younger, he hangs out with us, don't he? He's one of us" and all this, you know.

Q: OK, what else. Those were rough times. That's hard for a kid to have to deal with. So you were threatened sometimes and you had guys who stood up for you, because they were bigger.

Santangelo: I had that, even in the Army, the same way. Even in the Army the same way. I went in the Army, and I was really afraid to leave home. Scared, first time. I was 18, like. I didn't want to leave. I knew I had to leave. It was like going into the world, like thousands of guys have done since then. But I was really a mama's boy. I mean, my father loved me, I loved my father, but my mother brought me up, you know, and she never let anybody push me around like.

There was this—well, I'll tell you this. There was this Irish family, and there were two brothers, and one, Michael, I'll never forget him. He was like a little nasty. He was nasty. Our families knew each other for years, the mothers and fathers, but he was a little nasty, and me being of Italian descent, he used to throw me "guinea" all the time, "little guinea, little guinea," and I hated that. And my mother and father hated that too. He called me that once, he dressed me down; when I say dressed me down, he sounded off on me in front of all my friends, you know. He's three years older than me, this fellow, you know. I think I was only about seven or eight at that time, and I went home, just like a kid, and I told my mother. I said, "Michael called me a little guinea."

"What are you crying about? " she said. I told her. I'll never forget it. She got dressed and she came downstairs, and she went right to him and she grabbed him and she said, "Listen, Michael, don't you ever call my son a guinea. You know, he's a boy just like you, he was born in this country." The whole bit she gave him. She said, "I know if I was to tell your father what you did, he'd box your ears, slap you around. I don't want to do that. I don't want to ever hear you calling my son a guinea again."

So I went upstairs with my mother. Next day I come down, he said, "You hadda tell your mother, you hadda tell your mother, huh."

I said, "Well, you hurt me, you hit me, you know—" He hit me in the arm when he did it. I said, "You hurt me and I don't like that name anyway. It's the only way to get you to stop. My mother didn't tell your mother."

"Good thing she didn't, I'll beat you up again," you know, like that. I said, "Oh yeah? Well, she made a promise that she wouldn't tell her, but you better not call me a guinea anymore."

So it's a funny thing, this guy today is a retired cop. And we're very good friends. I don't see him that often. But his mother's still alive. His father's dead. And my mother and his mother are still very close together. They're 78 years old, one month separates both mothers. Like he's retired now and he's got seven children. But I doubt he even remembers it today.

Q: The interesting—

Santangelo: But that was a thing, nationalities, in them days.

Q: It's important, huh?

Santangelo: Oh, the Irish, I was raised with Irish people.

Q: Not many Italians around?

Santangelo: Two. I think there was two of us in the crowd. All Irish. All Irish. I really knew them. I knew their songs, better than I knew the Italian songs. I knew words to Irish songs that are unbelievable, like people I meet today say, "How come you know the words of that song?" I say, "Well, I grew up with the Irish," which I did. Irish Americans. Not born in Ireland, but here. And they were tough kids, the Irish, they were tough. Paddy's day, they had their parade. We had no parade in them days. Columbus Day, you know. And the Irish, in them days, really always used the word guinea. It never was Italian. Only with some of them who had a little class would never refer to it, you know. A lot of them would tease with it and you knew they were teasing, but there were the ones that said it and you knew they meant it. It was always that way.

Q: Were other nationality groups around, or just mainly the Irish?

Santangelo: Well, in our crowd it was mostly Irish, two Italians, one Englishman and I think only one German.

Q: How about the rest of the area? Were you aware of other nationalities in the neighborhood?

Santangelo: Yeah, it was mostly Irish. Yorkville is made up of everything. It's a mixture, Germans, Irish, Italians, Polacks, and every crowd had their bit. But my crowd mostly was an Irish crowd.

Q: I see, you didn't know kids of Polish or German background?

Santangelo: No. Not really got into anything in them days about that. But I knew everything about the Irish.

Q: How important to your growing up apart from this—you've mentioned one way in which Italian was important to you, the way Irish kids or at least this one Irish kid would give you a hard time about it. But in addition to that, are there other ways in which being Italian was important to you in any way in your life? Was it important in your family?

Santangelo: Well, at one time I said to myself, "How come I'm Italian, I'm not Irish?" Everybody was Irish, you know what I mean? That's before I realized what the whole thing was about. But my parents never had any trouble speaking English.

Q: Did they speak Italian?

Santangelo: No. They spoke it very little to their parents. They never spoke it in our house. Oh no.

Q: I see, so you never heard Italian at home.

Santangelo: Never heard Italian in my house.

Q: But they knew how to speak it?

Santangelo: Very little, they knew the words to get by with their mother, with their folks, but the language was never spoken in my house. And I look furthest from Italian than anything. I was told when I was a kid even, and the other fellow was more or less on the darker skin type, the olive, and he was definitely Italian. You could look at him and know he was Italian. But I was always fair like, chestnut hair I had, real light skin like; no one would ever take me for Italian. But everybody knew I was Italian because that's the way it was in them days. They knew what you were. Not that it made any difference to the parents, between the parents. It's what it was between the kids. But in them days all Irish kids referred to any Italian kid as a guinea.

Q: The parish—Our Lady of Good Counsel was your parish, right? That was not an Italian parish?

Santangelo: No. If anything, Irish. If anything it was Irish. But you have to remember, Yorkville's made up of everything.

Q: Did your parents associate primarily with other Italian American people? There wasn't anything in your life that was organized around being Italian?

Santangelo: No way. No way.

Q: In church or the people that your parents saw or anything like that?

Santangelo: No. They had Italian friends, Irish friends, German friends.

But I would say mostly, in the area, it was Irish at the time that was here. There was the other, but the majority happened to be the Irish. Like I can remember, I can give you names like, and they're all Irish—Cane, O'Connor, Delaney, Norton, Coglin, Regan, these are all Irish names, McNulty—

Q: These are the people you knew?

Santangelo: Right. Cameron was the Englishman. Vegra was the Italian. I could give you all the names, you know. McGuinnity. Walsh. You can see, Heintz, that's the German one, but most of the names were Irish. McLynchie, a little Scotch Irish in there, Wallace, they were all—Byrne, these are all names—even the crowd from St. Ignatius was on the Irish side. Murphy, Dorman, Deevy. Toll was German, Ravis was German, Novarre was Irish, McLoughlin. Maffi was Italian. You see, if you notice, the Irish had an edge. That's why I say, Paddy's Day was so big in the city, I think. Even around this neighborhood yet today, it goes good.

Q: Germans you weren't aware of particularly in any great numbers here.

Santangelo: No. Not until later on in life, you know.

Q: Let's come to that another time. It's about 5 o'clock. Suppose we call it a day. That's fine—no formality between us—

Santangelo:—That's fine, Gerry—

Q: I sign my full name on the letter because it's an official letter, that we should have. But no, we're on a first-name basis, no formalities. Well, I don't know, how did you find this?

Santangelo: I didn't think the time would go this fast. I just hope it's interesting, that's the main thing, you know.

Q: It is. To me it's interesting. It is.

Santangelo: If you ask questions probably more will come out, you know what I mean?

Q: Yes, that brings out things that I'm thinking about, that I want to know about, that wouldn't occur to a person to think of on his own. Of course, I have a few more questions that I'll want to bring up, that I thought we might save for another time. Good. But you found it interesting, huh?

Santangelo: I did.

Q: Did you find yourself remembering things you hadn't thought of at all?

Santangelo: Oh, I sure did. I sure did. It's tough to start off with.

Q: Yes, it's hard because you're not used to it.

Santangelo: Just to get started sometimes. Then you find yourself rolling along and thinking things that just pop into your head. Then you say to yourself, "Gee, I don't know if they're going to be any use to you," you know.

Q: Well, you, don't you worry about that, see. Let me worry about that. I'd rather have more stuff than less. In other words, I'd rather have anything that you remember, and let me decide if it's useful or not—don't you try to decide whether it's going to be useful to me or not. At this point, everything you remember is useful to me. I'm really trying to—what—one thing I'm trying to find out is, what it is that people remember about their lives, you see, and the only way I can know that is if they give me their memories. So I'm really, that's one of the things I'm trying to find out, what do people remember about their lives at different times, their childhood, later in life.

Santangelo: The neighborhood—

Q: Yes, we've talked a little bit about that, the neighborhood.

Santangelo: The neighborhood in them days was great. They always say, you didn't have to lock your doors in them days.

Q: Is that right?

Santangelo: Sure. You know, I told you we had the bathroom in the hall, in my walkup flat, that you shared it with your neighbor, and we had a good neighbor, and I can always remember my mother coming in and saying, "Gee whiz, she didn't put any tissue paper out, it was her turn." And little things like that. Yet when I was going to school in the morning when I was a kid, my father used to come home like at 4 in the morning. Now, like I said, if he was half loaded, he would be going to the bathroom at 4 in the morning and fall asleep. Now, I'd be going out in the morning, 7:30, 8 o'clock to go to school, and I'd have to go to the bathroom. I'd have to knock on the door. Now, you have to remember, you have to open the door to your apartment, to reach out and knock on the door, waking up a man, saying, "Get up, I have to go to the bathroom." Meanwhile, he'd come in and just go right to bed. These walkup apartments, there was never a lock on the door. You never had to be buzzed into any door in them days.

Q: Amazing. It was a whole different world.

Santangelo: It was unbelievable, like that. I never heard of the word mugging until 20 years ago. You could walk down the street. My father came home 4 o'clock every morning, walked home. He didn't have to worry about anything. He had to worry only after the war, after World War II. But before World War II, he used to walk home. After World War II, somebody always used to take him home. He was getting older then, a little slower. But they used to walk him home. But you could walk through the streets. I mean, you knew everybody. The vegetable stand was always open 24 hours a day. He used to play cards with them two hours, pass the time, you know, if he wasn't tired from work, you know, he'd stay and play rummy till—two hours, till 6 in the morning. Daylight, he'd come up and go to bed.

But the iceman—everybody knew him. It was a different, I hate to say era, but it might have been a different era. I don't know what brought it into the world or into the city or what. I don't know.

Q: Where do you do most of your work now? You mentioned the first day we met that you were working on a job out in White Plains, or you had worked. Are you working there now?

Santangelo: I'm working right up here at Rupperts. I'm at the Rupperts site now, that's where I'm on.

Q: Just walk to work, I see.

Santangelo: Yeah. It's beautiful right now.

Q: You never had any desire to move out of this neighborhood, huh?

Santangelo: No. My wife did, but not me. She always wanted a house like anybody else. Any woman would, you know. But not myself, I didn't. I was very content being around my friends in the neighborhood, my mother.

Q: Your mother lives around here?

Santangelo: My mother lives five blocks away. I see her every day. She's getting up like in years now. I go to the stores for her and everything like that. It's convenient for schools for my children, they have their friends. My wife has her family here and everything like that. She's given up. Oh, she's given up on that.

Q: Decided to stay here.

Santangelo: Sure.

Q: OK, well, let's call it a day for today. Let's pick up another time, OK?

Santangelo: OK, Gerry.

Interview # 2
Interview with Francis Anthony Santangelo
by Gerald Handel

Q: I wanted to ask you a couple of questions about last time. One thing I wanted to get clear—the fellow that lives across the street that introduced you to St. Ignatius, Rooney was his name?

Santangelo: Charlie Rooney.

Q: I guess what I wanted to understand was, you lived right across the street from each other, but you went to Good Counsel and he went to St. Ignatius. How did that happen? Did people living in your block have a choice to go to one or the other?

Santangelo: Yeah, I guess it was mostly because of the parent situation, you know, how they felt. Like I think Charlie lived in the 80s before he moved up to 90th Street, and he must have started there and went to grammar school there, and he was familiar with all the boys down there and the priest in the neighborhood and everything like that, where I was only a block and a half away from Our Lady of Good Counsel, so it was like a neighborhood thing, you know.

Q: I see, so even though he was living across from you, he had started at St. Ignatius before. I was trying to understand how it was that two neighbors went to different parish schools.

Santangelo: Oh, yeah.

Q: OK. Another thing, I think last time we didn't talk much about your experience in the service. You mentioned it, of course. I wonder if you'd tell me about that, when you went in and just everything that happened in the service.

Santangelo: Sure, wonderful. Well, I went in April 23rd, 1945. I went into the Army. I was drafted into the Army. Both theatres of operations were still on. There was still war with Germany, still war with Japan at the time. I went to Fort Dix. I was in Fort Dix for, I got my shots and everything, and then they sent me down to Camp Gordon, Georgia, which today is known as Fort Gordon, Georgia. It's right outside of Augusta. I did 17 weeks of basic training down there in the infantry.

While I was in basic training, the war with Germany ended in May and the war with Japan ended in September. I came home on a ten-day leave right at the end of September. I was home for ten days, and when the ten days was up I went to Fort Meade, Maryland, and from Fort Meade, they put us on a troop train across the country to Fort Ord, California. We stayed in California for three weeks because there was no ship available to take us over. Then we got notice one night that we were going up to Fort Laughton, Seattle, which was an embarkation point, and from there we boarded a boat, held I think about 2,500 GIs. It took us 18 days to get to Japan, to the coast of Japan. We laid outside of Hiroshima while the officers on the ship went to inspect the damage that the atom bomb had done when it was dropped a month and a half before then. They got off the boat, and they came back and they gave us an orientation on what it looked like and everything like that. Then we were on the ship one more day, and we docked at Nagoya, Japan. From there I went to a small town called Hemiji, Japan, and then I found myself in the field artillery, because there was no need for any more infantry. The war was over.

My duties in the Army mostly consisted of occupation. Guard duty and making sure that the people didn't act up and everything like that. There were still people that were very hostile. They didn't know that the war was over—not that they didn't know it, but they didn't believe that it was over, because it was only like five weeks since the actual shooting had ceased.

I stayed in Hemiji for about three months. Then we were transferred to Tamiyoka air, seaplane base, which is between Yokosuka and Yokohama. It's a little—I don't know how to describe it, just a little seaplane base, and it had barracks there, and it was used during the war for the Japanese naval fliers, for mostly reconnaissance.

When I arrived there, I was put into the coast artillery. And I never even saw a coast artillery gun. It was just the idea of all this filling in the time now, and the base mostly was used as guard duty. The troops were mostly used for guard duty in Yokohama. They pulled six-hour shifts. They would work from 12 to 6, 6 to 12, and so forth right around the clock. There were four shifts.

I didn't pull any guard duty. Of course this is where my sports knowledge came in, the weather being over in Japan like always in the 70s, southern Japan where I was at the time, 80s. I ended up playing ball for the regimental team over there, which enabled me to stay out of the guard duty bit. But I still had to do some work, and I joined the communications department. I was more or less running the switchboard.

Q: Telephone?

Santangelo: Telephone switchboard, yes. And I used to work five hours a day, and every time there was a ball game of course if it conflicted with my duties, I would get off because of the ball playing, and I stayed there the other nine months. I really enjoyed Japan. I made a lot of friends with the people; they were very interesting and everything like that. The man is so domineering over there, it's unbelievable. Like the woman does all the work, and it's another world compared to our way of living. The girls and the women over there always wore sort of football pants. It looks like long slacks bloused at the bottom, like we used to wear knickers when we were kids. But the American way came in to these people after about six months when I was there, because then the girls started to wear skirts over there, and we realized that they did have legs just like anybody else.

Then I got orders to come home, and I left there after about a year, exactly a year I was there, and boarded a boat in Yokohoma. Ship was 11 days coming back because there was no mine fields like there was when we went over. Came back to the same Seattle. Got on a troop train, same way, five days across the States, back to Fort Dix, New Jersey, three days waiting for the discharge papers to become final, and I was out of the Army in late December '46. That was the termination of my Army career, just shy of two years.

Q: Tell me about some of the personal experiences you had when you were in the Army. You covered where you've been, your training and activities, but tell me something about the personal experiences that you had.

Santangelo: Well, I'll tell you, being down in Georgia, and being away from home for the first time in my life, it taught me how to come like, more or less to depend upon myself and not somebody else looking after me all the time. I guess it's like the beginning of my manhood, too. Learning to be on your own. I had a mother that always did everything for me, made my bed and gave me nickels and dimes when I wanted candy and went to the store, but now I was on my own. Now I had to watch my money, shine my shoes, take care of my clothes and more or less look out for myself. And it taught me a certain bit of independence like. I had to rely on myself. No one was going to do it for me, I had to do it for myself, and it really helped me a lot in life, my Army career—no matter how short it was, I mean it was not much of a combat deal, but just being out by yourself—like I say, I was only 18 years old at the time. I didn't want to go in the service. But after I was in it—and when I got in it, I knew I had to do it, and I accepted everything, and I met some very interesting people in the service, people who didn't want to be in the Army, people who did want to be in the Army, people who were trained—we were trained like to kill and everything like that in the beginning, before the war had ended, and how some people looked at it, like it was a way of life. And me being only a kid, I couldn't accept this, like I thought it was just like going to school, you had to learn this and learn that, but there was another thing to it, and I just didn't realize it at the time, how important it was, how the training was going to save my life if it ever came about. But I met some very interesting people.

Q: Can you tell me about some of the people that you remember most, that you met?

Santangelo: Well, I remember this fellow called Ayers, Lew Ayers his name was, and he was a southerner and very hardnose backwoodsman like, you know what I mean? I don't think (as the old saying goes) he knew what a pair of shoes was, until he got in the service, you know. But he was very bitter toward the Northern people like. I think he was still fighting the Civil War. And he didn't trust New Yorkers or anybody from New Jersey or up north. But like I say, when you live with somebody 17 weeks you get to know them a little bit, and he was very much to himself like for about seven, eight weeks, for the first two months, and then finally he loosened up. He found out that everybody else was human just like himself, and just, that he was brought up probably in trying times in the South in them days. He was from a farm, and he just used to get up in the morning at 5 and do farm work. He never knew hardly what a newspaper was like and everything like that. He was really like a backwoodsman. But he came around and we got to become pretty good buddies. We stayed all through the war together, what was left of the war, I should say. He went over to Japan with me and we became very good friends and we corresponded for a while, and then it just tailed off like, you know.

Q: Was he the only southerner in your outfit? Mostly a New York, New Jersey outfit?

Santangelo: Well, it was comprised mostly of northerners, and we had a few southerners in there. He wasn't the only southerner, you know, but it was funny how they looked toward the black people like. There was no black people in our outfit then. The blacks at that time were separated and had their own thing. But we had Spanish people with us. I could name you some, like Fernandez, Barrier, Lopez, from New York. They were New Yorkers and Puerto Ricans, and the southerners really looked on them and didn't really care too much for these people. But there was a fight once in the barracks over it, just an even-up match between my friend Ayers, in fact, had with this Fernandez fellow, and it was a shame. It was one of those things. And my friend took a beating. My friend took a beating that night. But they became good friends too. It was just a clash of personalities more or less at the time, you know.

Q: What about in Japan? Did you meet any Japanese people that you got to know at all?

Santangelo: Well, when I got to Japan, they had the usual workers in the camp, in the Army area, I mean. They would feed them, for working around the grounds. Like doing the GIs' wash and stuff like that. I met a fellow that used to drive for one of the official Japanese War Departments in Japan, in Tokyo, and he has a funny name. It's Nonoka. It's just like you would say, don't knock on the door. His name was Nonoka. He was a man about 57 at the time, and remember I'm only 18 at the time, and he was our houseboy, our room boy. He used to clean up the room and everything like that. We used to throw him cigarettes, chocolate or something like that. He had a family of five, and he wasn't a combat man, he used to just drive a general around, like I said, from Tokyo to Yokohama, all the cities, Nobe, Osaka, and his job was to—well, be a private chauffeur. So when the war was ended, he applied for a job on the U.S. bases like, and he was assigned to cleaning up the barracks. Well, we had two to a room at that time, and he was assigned to us, and he was just like the Japanese would give you the impression, always smiling, but you never knew what was behind their smile and everything like that. But I liked him a lot. And I didn't smoke cigarettes at the time, and I used to give him a couple of extra packs like for a tip, because the money was useless in that stage, because the occupation money was being printed for us to spend, so all that was around at that time was Japanese money. But he was—he had a dog by the name of Pinky, and he gave him to me and we used to keep him in our room, me and this fellow, Ayers, and we were very attached to him. He used to go down to the mess hall with us like that and we'd come out, we'd feed him what was ever left on our plates. But it just goes to show you the inexperience of a boy 18, a young man 18, not knowing like what was around you, because these workers had no food at all at that time, and they used to line up to get our waste that we dumped into the can. Like what I'm trying to say is, if we finished our mess and whatever was left over, a piece of bread, string beans, corn, we all dumped it, like today we do it in the garbage can, the same thing, only this was a clean garbage can and we'd dump everything in there, coffee, liquid, everything would be floating around. Now, all these workers had a foreman and he had a big can, and all the Japanese boys and men would line up, and he would dip this thing into the can, into the barrel where we had dumped our stuff and just pour whatever he came up with into these Japanese workers' cans. And this was their lunch. It really was sickening.

And yet when we'd come out, we used to like throw the—if we had a pork chop bone, if we had pork chops you know at the time or whatever it was, a little meat we had, we'd always save it for the dog—not realizing that there's human beings like looking at us.

Well anyway, needless to say, three days later, the dog was gone, and we believe the Japanese killed the dog and probably ate him or something like that.

Q: So this Nonok was one friend you made?

Santangelo: Yes, he was a friend to me. He used to point out different things, you know, but he didn't speak one word of English . It was very tough to communicate with him, but he saw how I was treating him like, like a human being, and I think he did my room a little extra special any time. You know, I would always give him an extra pack of cigarettes and everything like that and joke around with him, kid around with him. I'd never been to his house. I never met his family or anything like that, because we weren't allowed to go into different things. A lot of places were off limits to us, the restaurants and everything like that, because they thought they would be poisonous, early in the days of the occupation.

Q: So you didn't get into any Japanese houses.

Santangelo: I didn't get into any Japanese houses more or less until about six months after I was there; the last six months I was there, everything became looser, like the taverns, the restaurants, they became open. They were checked out by the medical department of the United States Army and they got a clean bill of health. But everything like more or less was off limits, even the so-called geisha houses were considered off limits then.

Q: You weren't supposed to fraternize with the women at all?

Santangelo: No, but plenty of boys did.

Q: I guess there were women around.

Santangelo: There were always girls of the street, and from the girl of the street there were an awful lot of cases of VD in them days. Because they had it legalized at one time. Prostitution over there was always legalized, and they used to, the department—health department, medical department over there always had an orderly and what was known as a pro station in them days, on the scene of the house more or less. And MacArthur, who was the head of the Allied forces there, after four or five months I guess he must have had too many letters from home from all these married people, what was going on, anything like that, I don't know how it was, but anyway he put all these houses off limits. And it's amazing, because the VD rate, before he put it off limits, was really nothing at the time. When he put them off limits, the boys were picking up girls in the street who were dirty and carrying the germ and everything like that, and it shot up about 50 percent more than it was, 60 percent, I'd say. They were just picking up anything in them days, you know. Although some of the GIs had their own girls. They used to just more or less like leave camp and go right to—to their homes, take care of the mother and father, give them some dollars or whatever it was to buy some food, and more or less would court the girl, and some of them ended up wanting to marry them in those days, which was the early days of the war. Now, this is only like two months, five weeks after shooting had stopped with Japan.

Q: Did you have a girl over there at any time?

Santangelo: I never had a girl. Never had a girl over there.

Q: I mean a steady girl.

Santangelo: No, I never had a steady girl.

Q: OK, how about your buddy Ayers? He didn't form an attachment either?

Santangelo: No, he wasn't—no, but he had went down to the houses of ill repute now and then.

Q: You didn't do that?

Santangelo: No.

Q: Weren't interested?

Santangelo: It never bothered me, more or less. I don't know whether I was too busy—like I said, I was playing an awful lot of ball. Japanese women were very nice, but I just couldn't see it, you know. And I wasn't, there was no hooks on me at the time. I wasn't married, engaged or anything like that.

Q: The ball playing, this was regimental teams competing with each other? You had a regimental league, or what?

Santangelo: Yeah. Each base had their own team. Like I was connected with the Tamiyaka seaplane base, and we had our own—when I say ball, I mean softball because baseball wasn't that big over there. And we used to travel to Tokyo, into Yokohama, Sake, Hobe, and play different clubs, and—

Q: Japanese clubs?

Santangelo: No, no, we played American servicemen. But the Japanese were very interested in baseball. They used to watch us and everything like that, and they loved—one thing they loved was baseball.

It all comes back, when I used to read about Babe Ruth, that back in the thirties, he went over there once, and he became such a big hit over in Japan, you know. He more or less introduced baseball to them and today they're very good at it.

Q: I remember that, when I was a kid reading there were touring teams in Japan that introduced baseball, American Big League—I guess Babe Ruth, Lou Gehrig, all those—

Santangelo: Lou Gehrig—they all went over there, and they popularized the game.

Q: So you always had a crowd of Japanese watching when you played?

Santangelo: All the time. All the time. And sometimes for practice, like if some of the fellows didn't want to, maybe it's warm and they want to go to a movie, it didn't get dark until like 7 o'clock, like right after chow, 6 o'clock, I would take some of the Japanese workers down to the ball field. I would take six or seven of them down to the ball field, and I would just bat and they would chase the ball, they loved it. I would bring gloves for them. They really could have went home but they stayed around to play ball. It was just like a bunch of kids. But I'm talking about like younger fellows too at the time, like.

Q: That's interesting, really interesting. What do you think your period of service meant to you in your life? What effects did it have on your life, as you look back on it?

Santangelo: Well, it cut into two years of my life, like it cut into everybody's life in them days. Like I say, my brother did 5, 5-and-a-half years or something like it, you know, and I lost two years, from 18 to 20. It really taught me a lot about people, how to treat people, how to watch your money, being out on your own, what it is to be without where you can't depend upon anybody and depend upon, just by yourself. It would be like being a bachelor today, I guess, having your own apartment, working, watching your money, gambling—you know, if you lose your last two dollars you have no money, you have to go borrow some. It gave you sort of independence. When I came out of the Army I thought I could do anything, like, by myself, go some place, just, I don't know, it was really a turning point into manhood for me like, you know what I mean? Like leaving my mother's apron strings so to speak and getting away and doing things on my own. Like she had said, "You're going to someday work for a living" when I quit high school, and she was right, of course, but this came after that, and it really taught me what I have to do in life is what I'm going to do for myself; no one's going to help me, I've got to do it myself, I've got to do it my own way. It's a form of independence, I thought.

Q: When you were in the Army you said you lost two years of your life, 18 to 20. Did you feel it as a loss, feel, "Gee whiz what the hell am I doing here. I'm losing time"? Or not? Or even now when you look back? How big a loss was it, would you say?

Santangelo: I figure I didn't lose a thing. At the time I'm sure I didn't want to leave and I was going to lose like two years, you know. But eventually I would have had to go, because of being in good health. I mean, I wasn't 4-F at the time, you know—but looking back, it's two years of my life that was just great. I mean, I saw things that, not because it was for nothing, but I wouldn't have crossed the country. I was in I don't know how many states, Georgia, Maryland, California, Washington. I went to a foreign country. I mean, I would always love to go back to Japan even today. I always said it to my wife, if I ever had the money or something, I would love to take a trip back there, just to see the changes that have been in the last 25 years. And it's going on 26 years now since I've been back there, and I would love to go back to that country. I really love the climate, the people are fine, to me, everything like that. What they did and everything in '41 was something else. That was their superiors who did all that, I mean, you know—I'm not justifying it. I love Japanese people. I mean, they were nice people and trusting people, their ways of life and how they did things, how hard workers they were, how—well, you can see today, how they're in with the Sony television and everything, half of our foreign stuff comes from Japan today, you know. But I would really love to go back there. I really enjoyed the Army life, even meeting my southern friends, who were very hostile to us at the time.

Q: OK, that's interesting. Let me pick up something else that's a little bit related. You mentioned last time that when you went into the service, you had been going with a girl, and she started going with your best friend, and then when you came back out of service, she was engaged to marry him. I'd like you to tell me a little about how long have you known him, what had been your relationship before then.

Santangelo: My best friend's name was Jimmy Donnell. And he was a year older than myself, and he went naturally a year before I did, and got out of the service about six months before I did. And we had the same thing in common. We played a lot of sports and everything like that. Now, he went into the Navy and I went into the Army. I was overseas when he came back, and he picked up the relationship with the girl I was going with at the time. Helen was her name, the girl that I was madly in love with in them days. Now, I guess they hit it off or whatever it is. They became compatible, because they ended up getting married. But I didn't know a thing about this when I was overseas. Her letters were getting, like instead of one every three days, it became one a week, one every ten days, and I even mentioned it in one of the letters. I remember saying, "How come you're not writing?" and she kept telling me about all the different fellows who were coming back from the service then. So and so was getting out this week, so and so the next week and everything.

She mentioned that Jimmy's out, but she never mentioned that she was going out with him or anything like that, just that the crowd was around and they all did the same bit, talk and kid around.

But a different era had come in, because now, this is two years later; now we're hitting the bars too, the taverns, they're drinking now, you know what I mean? There was no drinking when you were 17—you weren't allowed in the bar till you were 18. But in the two years, now I'm 20, she's 20, my friend is 21, they're having a few beers, and it's a different story now. There's no more ice cream parlors on the corner, candy stores. Everybody's going to the bar. And they used to dance and all that and have a ball.

Anyway, they got to know each other pretty well. I still didn't know a thing about it until I come home. The first night I was home, she came up to my house, and my mother tried to give me some sort of a hint—I brought an awful lot of stuff back from Japan, like souvenirs, pajamas, scarves, silk, everything was silk. I mean in them days everything was dirt cheap. I was getting silk shirts for $2 that would cost you today like $30. But I had bought her like four pairs of pajamas, a robe, handkerchiefs, everything like that.

When I was opening these things up, before my girl got there, my mother says, "Are you going to give her all these things?"

I said, "Sure, why not?"

She said, "Keep something—you never know." She was more or less trying to tell me that Helen was going out with Jimmy, you know. But she didn't want to get involved, everything like that. She didn't want to hurt me. She figured, best let Helen tell me.

So after we had dinner, Helen came up to my house. I hadn't seen her like since I'd went away which was close to—well, a year and a half because I was home on leave. So I remember, we were in the front room. She kissed me hello, how are you, everything, so glad to see me. She cried, so happy I was home. We sat down. I started to give her some of this stuff, you know. So she said to me, "Oh, it's so much, you shouldn't do this," you know, all that.

I said, "Why not?" But I had no intentions of marrying this girl at the time, just that I figured she was my girl. Marriage never entered into my head, you know. So she had told me, then she said to me, "I just want to let you know—you know, I've been going out with Jimmy, and I like him very much, and I figure you might as well hear it from me, before you hear it from all your friends that you haven't seen yet."

So I was a little hurt by this, you know; I said, "Gee. Yeah?"

She said, "Yeah. It's nothing, it's just one of those things."

And like I say, when it come to girls, I wasn't too sharp. Put a ball in my hand, it was a different thing, but when it comes to this puppy love stuff or whatever it was in them days, I was really green to everything like that. So I was annoyed at it. I was very madly in love with this girl and I was very hurt by it.

So she says, "I'm not going to be your steady girl. I want you to know I'm seeing Jimmy," and everything like that.

So I said, "Well, OK. What can I say?" You know. So she left, and I think I had maybe two or three dates with her after that, just like soothing over. She more or less agreed to go out with me at the time. Because a year later after I was home she got engaged to Jimmy and ended up marrying him. Today they have four wonderful children. They live out in Old Bethpage, Long Island. He's a retired police officer today, and he's still one of my best friends today.

Q: Oh yeah, you still see him?

Santangelo: I see them when they come back into New York.

Q: How old were you when you got to know Jimmy originally?

Santangelo: I met Jimmy when I was about 15, 16 years old.

Q: In school?

Santangelo: No, just neighborhood. From sports competition.

Q: He was on another team?

Santangelo: He was on another team. I played against him for one year. Then he joined us and he stayed with us. We became teammates.

Q: That's on St. Ignatius?

Santangelo: No, this is hockey; that wasn't baseball, this was hockey.

Q: I see, so you used to pal around with him.

Santangelo: Palled around with him at his house, my house, the whole bit, everything like that.

Q: Did he live in Yorkville?

Santangelo: He lived four blocks away from me at the time. Yorkville, 94th he lived. I lived on 89th then.

Q: Did he drop out of school?

Santangelo: Jimmy finished high school.

Q: He finished high school, then went in the Police Department.

Santangelo: When he come out of the service he worked for Western Electric. While he was working for Western Electric, he took the police force exam, passed it, became a police officer, and a very good one I understand, too, couple of medals and all that. But he wanted to get out, and when his 20 years was up, which was two years ago by the way, he retired, and now I understand he's going to school for television, to repair televisions, at night. Very handy fellow, Jimmy was.

Q: So he was your best friend in those years before you went in service?

Santangelo: Yes, he was very close to me.

Q: When you came out of service I assume that he wasn't your best friend any more, you had. . . . (off tape)

Side 2

Q: OK, this is the second side of the tape—one other thing I want to ask about from last time, if you could tell me a little more about Father Durney. You mentioned that he was a priest that you'd gotten to know. That was after the war?

Santangelo: After the war, Gerry.

Q: And you say he was important to you.

Santangelo: Yeah, became a very close friend of mine. Did an awful lot for people in the parish and everything like that, and was such a real good human being. I know that was his work, being a priest, to help people, but I mean he really went out of his way, had that air about him, that distinction bit, you know what I mean; you knew he was sincere like, not just going through the motions.

Q: What effect do you think he had on you? Any effect on you any way?

Santangelo: Well, I don't know how much of an effect he had on me in life. I mean, he became another—a friend of mine. He was an acquaintance, when I say this, he was an acquaintance, I knew of him. When I got to know him better, he really became a friend of mine. Like I went out of my way to make sure I could see him, dinner, hockey games, swimming with the kids, different things and everything like that. He helped me get more or less—if it hadn't been for him, I wouldn't have gotten involved with the kids, like manager, and help the Little Leagues.

Q: I see. Are you still doing that today, involved in Little League?

Santangelo: Well, I haven't done it in the last two years, Gerry. I got away from it a little bit. Kids grow up, you know, and they go on to different things. But I'm thinking about going into it next year again.

Q: I see. But it was through him that you got into it in the first place.

Santangelo: Yes. I always wanted to do it, you know, but I never pushed myself, and he said to me one day, "Tony, what's the matter? You've played ball all your life. Don't you think you could pass something on to the kids in this neighborhood who need it and they're looking for a leader" and all like that?

And he made me feel like, gee, I never considered myself like an instructor or anything like that who could pass anything on to kids, you know. And I took time out. I told my wife about it. And it meant being away from the house more too, getting up early on a Saturday, going over at 8 in the morning with kids, because that was the time we had the field, playing baseball with them, teaching them the fundamentals of the game, the sportsmanlike conduct and everything like that. I did the baseball teams for him, for the parish, and then in the winter I did the hockey teams and that was like traveling all over the city to play the different games and sports. It cut into my time. But I enjoyed it, and I know I was helping him out too, and he really appreciated it. He told me what a job I was doing and everything like that, and it was good to hear. You know, usually you're just doing everything, and you don't hear something, it just goes unanswered like. You don't hear "you did a good job." It's nice to hear now and then. Not that you're looking for it, but he always took time out to say, "Thanks a lot." He appreciated it, you know.

Q: I think everyone of us wants to feel appreciated; that's a human feeling we all have, so that gave you a good feeling. I guess it was all day Saturday, or Saturday afternoon? Did you practice Saturday mornings?

Santangelo: We'd practice, and then we'd have the game, and then we'd stop for sodas with the kids, and it took up maybe about four or five hours of my Saturday, you know. Working with the kids after school, calling practices.

Q: Oh, you worked with the kids after school too?

Santangelo: I used to have a practice twice a week with them after school.

Q: So I see, that really was a big chunk of your week.

Santangelo: And I called on some of my friends to help me out, which they came forward, but a lot of the fathers, you'd be surprised, are not interested in it and all that. They come out to watch the games, some of them, but a lot of them you don't even see. Well, you can't tell everybody what to do in this world, you know.

Q: That's true. How many years did you do this?

Santangelo: I did this for almost ten years, eight to ten years, around eight years I'd say, eight years full time at it. Full time. I got away from it too, and I intend to go back, because right now they're starting to build a hockey field around here and I want to start these kids. They know how to play the game, but I just want to get a Little League started, keep them organized, and play other parishes.

Q: Is this ice hockey?

Santangelo: No, this is roller; there's not enough ice in New York for us.

Q: Roller hockey.

Santangelo: Which is a very big program around this neighborhood.

Q: OK, that's interesting. That fills it out. You still see Father Durney occasionally?

Santangelo: I'm a little ashamed of myself. I haven't seen him in three months now, and I've got to get on the phone and call him and have dinner with him.

Q: OK. Let me ask you another kind of question now. I'd like you to think back over your life, and think of some of the difficult times that you've had, some of the problems. How did you get through these times and what effect do you think that had on you? Let's start with the earliest one you can remember. A difficult time as a kid.

Santangelo: (Inaudible).

Q: I asked you about the best times in your life, but I don't think I asked you this. What ways do you think you'll change in the future? How do you think you're going to change?

Santangelo: Well, I'll tell you, changing in the future, I don't know—maybe giving more time to my family, like, you know—I told you, I've always been a selfish guy. I mean, my family comes first to me in responsibility and everything like that, but sometimes, for devoting time to them, if there's something for me to do, like if there's a ball game, I would play that ball game, other than take them on picnics. Now, like I say. I'm getting older and everything like that and I'm not saying my family was second in that, you know, because I always took my kids to the zoo and things like that. I think I've been the average father you know, taking them here, taking them there. I've given them enough of my time. But I think this. But naturally my wife thinks I should have gave more. In that respect, my kids are growing up, my daughter like I say is 18; pretty soon, God willing, she'll be married you know, meet somebody and get married. Now I only have my boy, who's already 16, and how long is he going to stick around? So the only one I really have left is my baby, and she's seven already.

I don't know, maybe, might get to know my wife better or something. Maybe the two of us didn't get away enough together, you know. And stuff like that. I mean, we understand each other perfectly and everything like that, but we really don't get away by ourselves like we should. It's up to me more or less to make an effort now and say, "The hell with this," say, "Let's go. Mom, you and I are going away for a weekend." I know she's dying to do it, you know. A little more attentive toward the relationship I'm gonna have with my wife the rest of my life. Let's face it, after the kids go away, it's just going to be the two of us, just sitting around the house. I don't know, I don't like to think about them days, to be honest with you, because I still have my children now, you know, and they take up a great deal of our time. I wish I had three more, to be honest.

Q: You haven't had a chance to get away with your wife for a weekend before.

Santangelo: No. Not really. Money problems. Little different things, you know.

Q: That's something you have to do in the future.

Santangelo: Yeah. I mean she went away for the summer. She goes away for the summer and I go down there for the weekends and you know, but—

Q: Takes the kids?

Santangelo: She takes the kids down there, but it's just like being a babysitter all over. I just like to leave the kids home and just get away. Even if it's only a weekend. Naturally I'd like to take a cruise with her some day, I mean, which is in the future, maybe when I'm 25 years married.

Q: OK. What ways do you think you're going to stay the same?

Santangelo: Well, I don't think anything could change my ways. I guess I'm more or less set in my ways now. Just what I'm doing. I mean, there's nothing more in life I think I can do. I mean, I get up in the morning, I go to work, I come home, now and then I stop into the bar or the tavern, see my friends, have a drink or two, come home, have dinner, watch television with my wife, go to bed, get up in the morning—it's more or less the same routine.

On the weekends I take my baby out maybe to the zoo or the park or something like that. I don't do this every Saturday. My wife will do the shopping, then Saturday night maybe we'll go out, meet some friends of ours, go to a tavern, have a drink or two. Sunday, same bit, get up in the morning, church, go home, play ball. My wife comes up and watches me play ball. Then she comes home. If it's too late we go out and have dinner. If it's not too late, we go home and eat. And television. It's not really an exciting life.

Q: You all go to church together.

Santangelo: Yeah.

Q: You go pretty regular?

Santangelo: Pretty regular.

Q: So as a person, your way of life you don't think will change much, and you as a person, you think you're going to stay pretty much the same?

Santangelo: Yeah. The only change that's come into my life that has been big was about a year ago, like I say, when the store was sold, the tavern where I worked for 16 or 17 years, and I became more or less into the whole new field of the building line, the construction line, going back into the construction field. Now, this is 17 years later. I'm older. The work is tough. Its outdoors. This is the only change I see in my life, like meeting all new people, more or less. Let's face it. I'm getting tired. You know, you get up early, you come home, you're tired, there's not much you could do. The pay is good and the hours are short, but the work is hard, and you're subject to all kinds of weather.

Q: The hours are short; what do you mean?

Santangelo: Well, seven hours a day.

Q: Seven hours and that's it. Sometimes there's some overtime?

Santangelo: If there's overtime, which is rare, there's overtime, but my hours consist of 8 to 3:30 with a half hour out for lunch.

Q: Five days a week.

Santangelo: Five days a week. It's 35 hours. It's a great job.

Q: OK, all right—now, I'm asking you to think about the things that have happened to you, and the kind of life you've had—I'd like you to think about this. What opportunities would you say you've had in your life, opportunities that came your way?

Santangelo: Opportunities that came my way? Well, I guess the biggest opportunity that ever came my way was when my father had that Sanitation Department test for me to take, you know, had that job open for me, and I didn't take the job. Of course we went over that. But that was a great opportunity for me; that would have meant security and everything for my family, retirement and everything like that, and I went on to a job which offered me nothing after that. And now I'm in a job which does offer you retirement after a certain age, I mean, but not like the city does. It's all your own money that you pay into this. But I have to do 20 years in this, and you gotta remember, I started doing this at the age of 44, so to be eligible for that, I have to wait till I'm 64. Now, I already told you about my best friend Jimmy Donnell, who took the police test. Jimmy is 47, same age as me, and he's already retired. I have a long way to go till I can do that.

Q: There was no retirement when you were working at the steak house.

Santangelo: No. No form of retirement, because it was a business, and if business went bad, which it did, everything was lost. There was no money compensated or anything like that. All I got out of it was two weeks pay.

Q: So now when you say you've got to put your own money in, what is it, a union pension fund?

Santangelo: It's a union annuity fund, they call it, like, you know. So much of your pay goes in, so much by the hour. I think it's $1.02 or $1.04 an hour goes into an annuity fund.

Q: The employer doesn't put any in?

Santangelo: The employer pays that. He pays that to our annuity.

Q: Oh, I see, you don't get anything deducted from your pay.

Santangelo: No, I don't get nothing deducted from my pay for that. But like before I could even touch that, which no one touches until they really need it, like a case of emergency—and I don't really have anything in there to touch, after only a year and a couple of months working in the business like. I mean, my annuity now is probably something like $802 or something like that, which is nothing. But if I wanted to borrow on that, I could only get half of it. That's the way the rules go. I could only get $400, and to borrow on that you have to have a case of emergency, a death in the family or you're buying a house or something like that or buying a new car, or a co-op apartment. And I don't want to touch that anyway because I figure, while I'm in good health and good shape, the idea is to work and build it up for the day when I can't go to work. That would be the main thing. Give my family some sort of security out of it.

Q: What about the apartment here? How long have you been living in this?

Santangelo: In this project? I been living here eight years.

Q: Was that something you had to apply to get into?

Santangelo: I applied to get in here eight years ago. My wife pushed me to do it. I didn't want to leave the apartment I was in. She said, "Let's go, we've always lived in a walkup flat. I'm tired of stairs. They have elevators down here. It's a city project. We'll be in with all types of people. A lot of our friends are going in. The church is pushing everybody more or less for this. They want to keep the neighborhood" and everything like that.

I said, "OK." We were one of the last ones to get an apartment in here, which was like eight years ago, and definitely it was the best thing that ever happened, because I never knew, if you remember, I never knew what it was to have a full-tiled bathroom, shower, steam heat, 24 hours a day, all modern apartment and everything. It was really great.

Q: You never had that in the other place?

Santangelo: Never had it any other places I lived in. Oh, we had steam heat later, you know, but a real modern apartment, like these things are only built nine years ago, you know, and we got in here 8 1/2 years ago. We were like one of the first ones in. Like, no one's ever lived in my apartment but me. Like I was the first one to go in there, like it's mine, like I've done so much for it, you know what I mean? I live on the 23rd floor. I've got a beautiful view of the river. I mean, it is fantastic. It's something that should have happened to this neighborhood 20 years ago, 30 years ago.

Q: You're really happy here.

Santangelo: I'm very happy here. The area is, I wouldn't say it's deteriorating, but it's right on the borderline of Harlem, more or less, East Harlem, 96th is the borderline. We have our trouble occasionally with different groups that come down here, the mugging in the elevator, the purse-snatchers and everything like that. We have patrolmen that walk the grounds, city housing. People say they don't do the job. There's five buildings here. Now, I don't know if they can cover the whole five, but to be honest, I don't see them sometimes, and they should be out more, I think myself. But they're supposed to have an undercover force that's started here now, plain clothes, walking around.

The area isn't that bad. But there have been holdups. There's nothing like security. I mean, I am a tenant patrolman myself. One night out of the month, I donate my time, three hours. I stay on the door with another partner of mine, another tenant, Frank Hunter, and we do one night a month from 8 to 11 o'clock at night. It's Tenant Patrol Security Guard, and you'd be surprised how the old people are glad to see us in that hallway between 8 and 11 at night.

Q: Makes them feel a lot more secure, I'm sure.

Santangelo: Right, and some of them say "thank you" which is always nice to hear, because you are giving up your time. We're not getting paid for this. And if more people in the building would do it, more of the fathers or the men you know who live there, you would really get it only once every two months. But because they don't turn out, we have to do it once a month. There's times you say to yourself, "Gee, I had a hard day, I don't want to go down there" and then you say to yourself, "Gee, you've got kids and anything could happen" so you pick yourself up and you go down there and you sit and more or less talk to your partner and see that the hall is clear.

And we've been doing this now, the Tenant Patrol has been in effect down here six years now, and we haven't never had any trouble in the hall. In fact, since the Tenant Patrol has been on, I think, there hasn't been no purse snatching or muggings or anything during the hours of 8 to 11.

Q: OK, in a way, getting this apartment was an opportunity, knowing about it, I guess. Not everybody knew it was possible to apply here. Do they have certain income limits or qualifications for getting in, or how do they?

Santangelo: When they first started here, they had an income limit. It went on your salary, what rent you would pay at the time. Now, since then of course, with times changing, salaries getting higher, if you make over x amount of dollars, I really don't know the figures, they raise your rent. So when I first moved in here, I was paying $85 a month. That's eight years ago. Unheard of because I left an apartment that I was paying $87 a month. I came here for two dollars cheaper, and I got all these conveniences of an elevator apartment and running water with force, not waiting to see your neighbor isn't using the hot water to let it run up. But now today I'm paying $96 a month. I've had an increase of $11 in eight years, and my apartment without a doubt is worth at least $125, $130 a month today in New York, easy, at least.

Q: You have a couple of bedrooms?

Santangelo: I have three bedrooms. I mean. So—but I'm just talking about that it's in a project. If it was in a private house of course it would be worth like at least $220, $250 a month.

Q: Oh yes.

Santangelo: But we have three bedrooms. The reason for the bedrooms is because of the opposite sex in the children. I have one boy and they had to give us the extra bedroom for him.

Q: Right. Sure.

Santangelo: But now, with my going into this other business now, leaving the bar business, my salary has jumped. See, every year you have to fill a form in for the city, on what you make and everything like that. Now I am going to be raised probably some money in my rent. How much, I don't know. It might be $2, it might be $15, but we're all set to accept it because we figure, in the area, all our friends—a lot of our friends have moved away from this area, saying the neighborhood was going and everything like that. They've bought houses 50 miles away on the Island, 40 miles away in Jersey, and they say they love it. Well, I think you really have to be cut out to have a house and accept that way of life. If you can spend yourself traveling an hour and 20 minutes a day one way, which is two hours and 40 minutes, just for traveling—it's not for me. Believe me it's not for me.

Q: Let me ask you a different kind of question. What do you think you've learned from your own life, things that have helped you as you went along? That's a big question, I know.

Santangelo: I've had so many experiences. I believe I've had, you know. My Army experience taught me more or less to stand on my own two feet in life. Then I've met different, all walks of people in the Army, you know, southerners, how they thought—I never met a southerner in my life until I went in the Army. I never knew they was still fighting the Civil War. Then, coming out of the Army, going into the bar business with my uncles and what a way of life. What an education. Anybody who really wants to get to know people should always deal with the public, like be a waitress, if you're a woman, if you're a man, be a waiter. Just mingle with the public, where you have to cater to them, you know, and it's like, when you go out yourself, you want somebody to wait on you. You want the best and everything like that, and you see cranky people, you see rich people, you see poor people, the people that can't afford to go out—you meet so many types of people it's unbelievable. And it's all a lesson to you, I think, you know. You see how the rich guy goes, how the middle guy goes, and how the poor guy goes. The poor guy struggles to take his wife out and spend a dollar on her, and she's tickled pink to go. The middle class guy goes, and we might do it in two weeks, and it's accepted, where the rich guy, it's an every night affair and oh, let's go some place else. You see all walks of life and you say to yourself, gee, you never knew that things like this existed with people. I never did anyway, you know what I mean? That's just what I'm talking about the restaurant, like people coming in, and I learned a lot about people there and that influenced me. I always believed I would do the best to my means to go out and take my wife out here or there, you know. And I always believed that you should take your wife out.

I hate to get on wives now, but I'm talking about like what it—the influence it had on me, seeing this. You have to devote something other than just going home every night and just sitting around and listen to the radio or television or reading. You have to make an effort to get out together and keep that companionship going, you know. I really found this out by the bar business, because before I went in the bar I'd just come home, we'd hang around, go for a drive or something or go to a movie. But I mean, going out and socializing with people. I had a lot of friends all my life, but I mean, mingling with different people. I met so many different people in the bar business, it's unbelievable.

Q: Do you go out more with your wife since you were in that?

Santangelo: Oh, we socialize much more now. I have an awful lot of friends. A great couple who's very close, the Shanahans, we go out for dinner an awful lot, you know, or we go to dances if the neighborhood clubs are having them. If they have a bus ride, we make a special thing to make those things, you know. The only thing that stops us from doing anything is like a sickness to one of the kids or something like that. But we go to house parties.

Oddly, we don't go to the movies enough together like we should, because we don't agree on movies—like, my wife, not saying she's a prude, but she doesn't like some of these movies they're making today, like "The Exodus" and stuff like that, you know. I didn't see that but I've seen other pictures, and the language barrier is, my wife really doesn't go for it. And I tell her, "Well, I have to see these because I just want to stay up on things," you know, like "Serpico" and stuff like that. I already told her what "Serpico" is about, and she knows the whole story, and she says, "To hear those words in the motion—" it's not worth it for her, she just refused to go. So more or less I pick out the movies to go, like the "Sting" and stuff that's more or less PG rated, and she goes with her sister more or less. We go occasionally to a PG movie, but there's too many other kind around that are violent. She's not much for violence, my wife. She really doesn't go for violence.

But our social lives with other people, we do pretty good, I'd say.

Q: You have people in to your house?

Santangelo: Occasionally we have them in. We should have them in much oftener, much more, like, to be honest with you. I just mentioned that the other day. But she's like all women, you gotta paint this, you gotta straighten that out, you know, and she wants her house to be immaculate. I said, "This is our home, they like us or they don't like us; you're not living in a pig pen." But like a woman, everything's got to be in the right spot at the right time.

Q: She feels the house, your wife feels the house doesn't look good enough? That's why she doesn't want to have people in more? She wants everything to be just so, is that it?

Santangelo: Yeah. She really goes overboard when she has company, like you know what I mean? She'll break her back for three days getting ready for a Saturday night in that house, and I'll say, "Catie, they're our friends. I know you have to do a certain amount of cleaning but don't go crazy. You 're knocking yourself out. When the party comes, you'll be out of it; it'll take you two weeks to recuperate from it."

Q: Is this a dinner party, or after dinner?

Santangelo: After dinner, coming up for a few drinks, you know, some midnight snacks, more or less general conversation and talking.

Q: She wants to really do a thorough job before—

Santangelo: When she does it, it's got to be 100 percent. Me, I'm different. I would say "Let's have it tonight" and take right from the bar. "Let's go up to my house and have a drink and sit," where she would die, if I did that.

Q: She really doesn't like you to bring people home if she doesn't know about it ahead of time.

Santangelo: Oh, she says, "Just give me a phone call." It's not that I can't bring anybody home, but just don't walk in cold on her, like. She could be folding wash or something like that, you know, different things. She'd just like to be a little tidy, you know.

Q: Right.

Santangelo: I guess there's nothing wrong with it.

Q: Well, every person has their own way, you know. I'm really just trying to find out how it works in your house, rather than, I'm not saying it's right or wrong, just trying to find out how it is.

Let me ask you another kind of question. Do you think your life could have been different in any way? Could you have become a different kind of person, do you think?

Santangelo: I don't really think so, Gerry. Maybe if I didn't get married, I might have become a different person. I mightn't have been married today. I might have been just bouncing around, going with everything, you know, girls. And this one one night, that one the next night, then just going home and going to work and spending money and drinking and—

But I think, as I say, I just refer back to the athlete situation. Sports had an awful lot to do with it, and getting married. If I didn't get married and have the girl that I have today, who knows where I would have ended up or what? My wife had a very big influence on my life I think. Yes, I think so.

Q: She did. What attracted you to her?

Santangelo: I'd like to know, today. No, she liked everything that I did. She liked sports. We were very compatible. We liked movies. We had a lot in common like that—you know. We really got along very well. She was a great dancer. I was horrible, and she followed me so good, I said I'd better marry her.

Q: Most people have had some problems in life. What problems would you say you've had? Maybe we've talked about some but maybe there are some we haven't. What would you say have been the problems in your life, that you've had?

Santangelo: Oh, I guess the problems in my life—let's see. Going back—being accepted when I—I was always a small kid, hanging out with all older fellows, and that was one of the big problems, like how to be accepted by this older crowd, and just by being myself you know. I guess they got to like me, and it was like a feather in my cap more or less, not being an outcast, you know, and stuff like that.

Q: How did it happen that you hung out with an older crowd as a kid? Were there no kids your own age at the time?

Santangelo: No. There was nobody my age in that block. Everything was blocks in them days, you know. You lived on 90th St. I lived right off 90th Street. Everybody hung out on 90th Street. The crowd that was there was always, like I say, three or four years older than myself. The kids that I went to school with came from different blocks, like two blocks away, four blocks away and everything like that. They all lived and they all had their own crowds more or less, you know. And when you went in them days two or three blocks out of your way to go to another block it was like going over the Mason-Dixon Line. Not that it was like a big thing. But you just hung close to your own house, more or less.

Q: I see. The block really was that important then.

Santangelo: Well, it was always a crowd of—it's not like today. Every block had their own crowd. Years ago. Today, they come from all over, just to meet, you know. But it was a different thing. Times were really different in them days.

Q: Tell me a little bit about your kids. What are they like?

Santangelo: Well, Nancy's my 18 year old. She was born '55. When she was a year old she was very sick. She had roseola and we almost lost her that time. It made my wife a nervous wreck, that sickness. To this day any time any of my kids get sick, she always thinks that she's going to experience what she experienced with Nancy—way back almost 19 years ago when we almost lost her. Nancy was in the hospital three days on the critical list. She was only a year and a half years old, and high temperature and everything like that, convulsions. But today if you ever seen this girl, you'd never believe that this could ever happen. But my wife, if my kids sneeze today or cough today, she's got them cough medicine—she's really, not over-mothering them but overprotection. Put on a scarf in the cold weather and everything like that. Don't drink out of the same glass that Jimmy drinks out of, he's got a cold. Marie's got a cold, don't drink out of her glass. She puts scotch tape on all the glasses with the names when the children are sick. They use special spoons in my house when they're sick, special knife, special fork, everything that's special, a plate that's special. And yet I can boil those dishes every night, she'll still put a piece of scotch tape on them and say, "Nobody eats off these utensils or plates other than the one who's sick in the house."

That's the way it's been for 18 years since Nancy got over that bad sickness that she had. But Nancy is a good girl. She grew up average young lady. She went to St. Ignatius, graduated from St. Ignatius; she went to Holy Cross Academy down on 42nd Street, Catholic High School. She graduated from there. We wanted her to go to college last year, but she didn't; she wasn't interested in it and she wanted to go out and get a job. She got a job, and she works today for a hair stylist. She's a cashier-receptionist. She likes her job because they're not too fussy about the way she dresses for work. She can go in her dungarees and everything like that. She works from 11 to 7:30. I have no idea what her salary is, to be honest, because my wife handles that. She says Nancy buys her own clothes and everything like that. You don't have to give her money, she's more or less paying her way. So that's Nancy.

Q: The rest of the money's hers. She buys her own clothes. She doesn't contribute to the house?

Santangelo: No. My wife tells me she's been taking $20 a week off her and putting it in the bank for her to save, and I believe she does that one week and maybe forgets the next week, because the way young ladies buy their shoes today, it's unbelievable, like $35 for a pair of shoes, where I'm paying $16 she's doubling me with these high heels and patent leathers they have and everything like that. But she's good in that respect, like she's home at reasonable hours. She gets a little lazy on Saturday and Sunday around the house. I believe she should help her mother more around the house, but she says she works all week and Saturday's her day of rest, and that's the only argument I have with her. I believe she should help her mother out a little bit more like, that. But she does the A & P if Catie has to do something, my wife; if she has to do something, Nancy will jump up and volunteer, and take the baby out to the zoo or something like that, if she has nothing to do.

She has a boyfriend. She's coming to another phase of life, you know. He comes over three times a week. He has dinner with us. His name is Doran. He's from the West Side.

Q: Is he Irish?

Santangelo: Hell, is he Irish, Danny Doran?

Q: Does that make a difference to you if he's Irish or Italian?

Santangelo: It makes no difference to me.

Q: Catie's Italian too?

Santangelo: Catie's Irish. My wife is Irish. I'm Italian. It doesn't make any difference to me as long as he's nice to my daughter. And he's a good kid. What I know of him. I mean, I don't follow them around at night, but what I hear, I have friends on the West Side and like none of them say I'm an overprotective father, but I've inquired about him, and he seems to be a good kid. Comes from a family of ten, by the way. So he knows what it is—when you see him sit down at the table to eat, he's not fussy, like my kids are fussy. He'll eat anything you put in front of him.

Q: You see that kind of difference, don't you?

Santangelo: Oh, you can see it, and how you can see it, Gerry. It really is something. It's a pleasure to have him at dinner, because I'll say, "Danny, do you want some of that?" He'll say, "OK." "Do you like —" He'll say, "OK." He doesn't refuse anything. I believe this kid will eat anything. It's really a pleasure to see him eat, and he cleans his plate. He won't take more on his plate, other than what he can finish. He doesn't become a hog, you know, or load his plate down, like my son will throw everything on it and walk away half—
I say, "What are you doing? Only put on your plate what you can eat."
"Well, I thought I could eat it, you know." He's a pain in the neck.

Q: Your son's 16.

Santangelo: 16, and a headache.

Q: Because of the eating or other things?

Santangelo: Oh, other things, like he's a real spoily, you know. I think he's so much of me when I was a kid, selfish, doesn't want to pitch in and do anything in to the house, like my mother never asked me to do anything. That's why I got running and coming and going like I pleased. Now Jimmy thinks he can do the same thing. He doesn't want to take time out if my wife tells him to do the rug. He makes a big scene, slams the door—I have to go in, grab him and threaten to punch his brains out, to get through to him that he has to do these things, you know. Meanwhile his hand is always out for money, "Gimme a dollar, I want to go get a soda and a piece of cake," you know, when he's out with his friends. Or "I'm gonna play ball and I'll be out, I wanta get a sandwich."
I say, "Jimmy, you get all these things, I mean I want you to have everything that I didn't have, you know, everything my father gave me, but just show appreciation, say 'Mom, can I do anything for you?' If you ever said those words to your mother, I think she'd drop dead."
But on the whole, he's a good boy. He goes to the Cardinal Hayes School now. His marks aren't the greatest. He's a little above the get-by stage, but he's playing hockey for Hayes and that's his incentive. I told him if his marks go down I'll burn his hockey sticks. And every time I threaten him like that, his marks go up. My wife says I should threaten him that once a week. But I do it once a month, you know. But I have to get on him a little more with his studies. He hates to take time out. I imagine it's his age. He's just running around like, enjoying life. I wish I was his age today.

Q: Does he ever think about what he wants to do? Does he ever say anything about that?

Santangelo: He hasn't said a word of what he wants to do when he grows up. I did this on my own. Last week, they had applications for the Department of Sanitation, and they want young people to take these. You have to be 16 to take this test. So I went and got an application for him. Friend of mine picked it up in fact for me. I brought it home. Jimmy mailed it in, and we got a card yesterday saying that he has to take the test March 2nd. Now, a friend of mine has a refresher course. You know, he took it, some notes, and he's going to lend them to me, and I'm really going to insist that Jimmy study this and takes that test and gets a decent mark, because they say it's going to be a waiting list of maybe two, three years. By that time he'll be out of school. He'll be 18, 19 years old, and if there's nothing around, the way times are today, a good job, and maybe he can get lucky enough to get on the DS, something that I turned down years ago. But I'm trying to get the importance of having a steady job into him while he's young, for his future, like security. This is the main thing that I want to try to get all my kids to know.

Q: You're really sorry you didn't take that DS job.

Santangelo: For security reasons, yes, you know. I am, really, more or less, when I look back, think back on it. Yet in a way I'm not, because I had such a good time meeting the people, the interesting people I met through all my life, though, being in the bar. And the acquaintances that I met, you know, all walks of life. I've met some beautiful people really. Really. Celebrities I've met, you know. A personal friend of mine is Art Fleming of Jeopardy. I don't know if you ever watch the television show. It's very educational. It's a quiz show. It used to be on at 12 noon. It's on at 12:30 in the mornings now. And he's a Cornell graduate, great man. He was down here on 85th Street. I met him in the old restaurant one day, and we got to talking. A real regular fellow like, nothing hoity-poloi about him, talks our language like, you know? Real nice fellow.

Q: You really appreciate meeting people like that.

Santangelo: Right. Right. And everybody isn't stiff, more or less or stuck up. He come in and had a beer with you and talked, you know, and "How's the show going?" He invited me down, not to go on the show but to watch the show and everything like that.

Q: Did you go?

Santangelo: I haven't went yet. The invitation's still open. He says, any time I want, I can go down NBC studios. He was the captain of the Cornell water polo team, which I understand he rates the third roughest sport going. He says hockey and lacrosse are the two above it, and pro football is fourth, in his eyes. I said, "Water polo? You gotta be kidding." He said, "Did you ever play water polo?" I said, "No." So then he told me about water polo, and it's funny, he says, "You know, you get a ball and you have to swim. I don't know if you're familiar with it, you have to swim and try to get it—it's like basketball." He said, "Then when you go under water, they hold you under water and they do everything."

"You know, Tony," he said, "I've got one tooth out of my head. I had it knocked out with an elbow in water polo. So anyone that says that water polo isn't a tough sport—"

But a real gentleman, very, real educated man, you'd really appreciate him.

Q: That's interesting. So you got a lot of good things out of those years at the bar, even though it didn't work out in the end the way you'd hoped.

Santangelo: Right. Some education, Gerry. People, all walks of life, alcoholics, priest would come in who enjoyed a drink, you'd be surprised. But I met a fellow from _____ Breweries. His name was Charles _____. He's the great-great-grandson of _____ Breweries, one of the brothers who opened it, and he is an alcoholic. They give him $10 a day allowance, more or less to go out and have some drinks. They can't do anything with him. They set him up with businesses, he blew everything, they sent him away. When he has to get the cure, they send him away to a farm and they cure him. He's married. He goes to London, England, European vacation once a year. They send him to Puerto Rico once a year, him and his wife. But they won't give him any money. They'll pay his bills. They won't pay any tabs in bars for him, and he's only allotted so much cash, and he says he wants to get a job, but you have to talk to him. You know he's lying, and he's trying to make the effort, meanwhile he's saying, "I'll have another Beefeater martini, make it dry."

But here's another walk of life, you know, a man with all this money and how alcohol has gotten to him—you know, like you read in the papers or television, a disease. It is, more or less. I really like Charlie. What a pain in the neck when he's loaded! Unbelievable. Oh. "Just gimme one more." It's a shame, you know, begging for that other drink, and I used to, here I'm shutting off maybe two million dollars, saying, "I don't care if you got all the money in the world, Charlie, I can't give you that other drink, because you're only going to get hurt."

And he'd leave there storming out, cursing me and calling me everything. Come in the next day like a lamb. "How was I, was I bad last night?" You know. All the experiences that you run across.

Q: Yes. It is in a way a great opportunity to see people like almost no other. One thing. I'm curious, did Catie work before you were married?

Santangelo: Catie was a bookkeeper for a company downtown. Jewish firm. Friedman, I think it was. She worked and then she became sick. She got sick. She got rundown. She had TB, my wife, and she was told by her family that she couldn't work no more because you know, tuberculosis, you had to take it easy, rest and everything. She was away for a few months, and she got her strength back.

Q: This was before you were married?

Santangelo: Before I was married, and she had the operation. She had a piece of her lung taken out. And then she got a job as a dental asistant. She worked one or two days a week. It all depends. She worked up at 125th Street for a Dr. ____, who had a big practice up there. It was a father and son practice. They had one office. Today they took over a bar up there and renovated it and they have I think seven dentists working for them. They have their own laboratory up there and everything. The old man has died, but when I was going with Catie, I used to go up and pick her up. I had a car in them days. I used to go up and pick her up. She worked Tuesday and Wednesday, or Wednesday and Thursday, whenever the girl would take off, you know. She would change her days to take off, and Catie would work the two days, because Catie couldn't work a full job 'cause it was too much for her. Her folks didn't want her to do it. Her whole family realized the situation and everything like that, and money wasn't that important. She used to work long hours for those two days. She worked ten hours a day up there. But she loved her job. Catie loves to work. And the old man really loved her up there. She would do the things that the regular girl couldn't do. She would dust and she would be doing all these little things, not just she had her teeth done for nothing and everything like that, but they became very good friends of ours, the ____. We don't see them, just when we go to the dentist, but we've sent half of this neighborhood up there. Even from projects where we live, all walks of life, up there. My children go up there, 125th between Park and Lex. He's still there, and very reasonable.

Q: Did she work until Nancy was born?

Santangelo: She worked; she left the job when she was six months pregnant. But that still was only that one day a week. I used to pick her up then.

Q: And she hasn't gone back to work since then?

Santangelo: Seven years ago she went to work for a company. She wanted to try her hand working again, before Marie was born, about nine years ago, and the job called for working from 4 to 12. It was mostly filing. She did it two weeks and was completely exhausted.

I said, "Have you had enough?" I let her do it, just to get it out of her system. More or less she's had enough. Although she's starting to come around with some hints now that she's ready again. But I think, I know what's on her mind. She has a lot of time now, during the day. My daughter works. My son's at school, the baby's at school now. So her free time consists of from 8:30 to 3:30. I think she's looking to pick up something like for three hours during the day, and personally I hope she does, because it will keep her a little more occupied, you know.

Q: So you're in favor of it, you're not against it?

Santangelo: Oh, I gave her my OK, because I believe it would be good for her, because it would keep her mind occupied. Not that she doesn't have enough to do, like with the laundry and taking care of the house. When you have three kids there's always something to do, picking up after them, you know. But I believe like, to keep another outside interest, even if it's only one or two days a week. She's got my approval, as long as it doesn't interfere with her health.

Q: Yeah, well, that of course is the important thing.

Santangelo: Because I wouldn't want anything to happen like what happened to her 23 years ago before we were married.

Q: But she's sort of getting interested—

Santangelo: —yes, because my wife isn't a strong woman, like she's smart, a very intelligent girl, but I mean she's really not built that strong, because that TB bit really knocked a lot out of her. She gets tired fast like, you know. She can be doing housework, heavy, and I'll say, "Why don't you stop?" And if she does it too much, it shows on her the next day. She'll just sit around, and I'll say, "What did you do that for?" "Well, I wanted to get it over with." Like getting ready for Christmas, she knocks herself out shopping. I tell her, "Don't do it, you're going to hurt yourself," and everything like that. She's had some serious operations since we've been married. I'm not saying it was because of that, but I think it helped slow her down a little bit. She had a very serious operation like four years ago. She had an infected ____, and they thought it was appendicitis, and when they opened her up, the doctor said she didn't have an appendix. She's one of these few people that don't have it. But the pain, she was diagnosed by three doctors that she had appendix. When they opened her up, they found inflammation there, and they said, "There must be something." They asked permission if they could go—I said, "Of course." They found a ____, and they said, if they'd closed her up that day or night, whatever it was, like within two days, peritonitis would have set into her whole system and she might have been gone.

But she had major surgery. She went up for a 45-minute operation for appendix. She stayed up there 3 1/2 hours under major surgery. She was in the hospital 20 days, 18 of them on intravenous. She had a very hard time. So I mean, she's had her real ups and downs, you know. Her whole plumbing system is all fouled up. She has no ____ now, she only has the ____. Everything like that. She says when she dies she's going to give her body to science because when they see this maybe they'll help somebody else. You know, she's very good people like that. But she's had it more or less rougher than I ever thought of having it.

Q: Well, I guess it works out that way for some people. It's too bad. But hopefully that's the end of that.

Santangelo: Oh, I hope so too. But the three children were born normal like, no complications with that or anything, thank God.

Q: You say Catie's Irish. Is she involved at all with Irish things? Is being Irish important in your family?

Santangelo: Let me clarify what I mean by Irish. She's Irish American. Anything that comes over on the boat now is a completely type of Irish to the Irish people.

Q: I understand, I was thinking just in terms of Irish background.

Santangelo: No, that's all right. She'll take the kids to the St. Paddy's Day parade like anybody else will, you know. Even the baby says, "I'm Irish." Catie will say, "You're also Italian," you know.

Q: Does being Italian play any part in your life today at all? You're not involved in any Italian groups, clubs?

Santangelo: None at all. None at all. And I am not—it's a funny thing, my wife is Irish and she makes an Italian sauce better than my mother did. And my mother was like I say, her mother was from Genoa, Italy, and everything like that, and my mother has to be the poorest Italian cook you ever saw in your life and my wife is the greatest. Myself being Italian, I am not a big Italian eater, yet I will eat the standard spaghetti and the veal cutlet parmigiana and everything like that, but my wife thrives on it. She loves to make the sauce five hours and everything like that, and my daughter takes right after her.

Q: That's interesting. How about your brother, was he more Italian? Or it didn't figure in his life, the people he went around with?

Santangelo: No, Big Tony was—like I say, we weren't that close, with the war and everything like that, but he hung out with anybody who was around, Irish, German, Polack or anything like that. He married an Irish girl also.

Q: He did. We were talking the other day about Yorkville. I think in the popular mind, people who didn't know much about it thought of Yorkville as being full of a lot of German people, of German descent and so on. When you were growing up, was there a German feeling around—the kinds of activities, stores, newspapers, music, all that around? Was it German, or you didn't have any impression like that?

Santangelo: Well, I'll tell you, Yorkville, as I remember it, was always known to be the German section of town, German American, right, 86th Street always had the German restaurants. They used to play the German music outside and everything when I was a kid.

We had an Italian restaurant on 86th Street too. We had a Blarney stone for the Irish on 86th. But everything, the majority was German.

Today it's almost the same way. It's still controlled by the Germans more or less, 86th Street, which is a big transit street. It's a cross-town street. They have the Steuben Day Parade today, which breaks up right on 86th Street right outside of all these German restaurants. They have an October beerfest which is always on 86th Street—Bock beer, always on 86th Street.

But as for German-American, Irish and everything like that, it had no big thing on my life. All I could say is that when you went to 86th Street you knew you were going, that's where the Germans were, but I mean, it was just elderly.

Everything was elderly. The Germans were to me, like, they always had the restaurants and the beer halls. I think there was a few German kids that hung out with us like that, but it was not a big thing. Everybody was accepted the way they were.

Q: You wouldn't even know if somebody's German. You know somebody's Italian, you know somebody's Irish, but you didn't know if somebody was German or not.

Santangelo: No. You didn't care, I think. I can't remember hardly anybody saying "He's a heinie" like they would call an Italian guy a guinea, I never heard anybody called a heinie, a Dutchman or anything like that. That was another phrase, Dutchman, like the Irish were called micks and everything. There wasn't that many. There wasn't that big a difference.

Q: Yorkville's changed a lot do you think since you were a kid? What changes do you see?

Santangelo: I think this section of the city is just about the same as it's been for the last 30 years. All I can see is East Harlem coming down closer. When I say East Harlem, I mean the colored people are coming down. They're drifting down now. More or less into 86th Street. Years ago, they had their own theatres, up there around 116th Street and everything like that. I think they've been torn down, so their movie houses will be [be]coming our movie houses like on 86th Street, like the RKO today up on 86th Street next to Gimbels—all it runs now is colored movies. "Shaft," "Five on the Black Hand Side" and everything like that. My son goes and sees some of these movies. Of course, their violence, he loves the violence with the detectives and everything like that. But more or less, the area itself has always been one of the best on the East Side. Today they say the West Side is completely shot. They're going to build up and everything like that. But if you take a general consensus of an area, you'll see I think that Yorkville people haven't changed, but what's changing Yorkville is these high rises that are going up. They're pushing the regular tenants, the walkup people out, the old Yorkville people out, forcing them to go to Queens, the Bronx and different sections, because they can't afford these high rises. They can't get into this project where I live because there's so much people waiting to be called for it. The best thing that could happen for Yorkville is for another two buildings to go up, to keep these people here, these regular Yorkville people here that have been here for years. Like in these high rises we're getting the Madison Avenue men, the businessmen, the ones that make the commercials. We're getting the airline stewardesses. We're getting bachelors that share an apartment. That's what you're getting in these high rises. There's no families in there. Can't afford it.

Q: I see. Well, I think at the moment, I don't have anything else to ask you, unless there's anything else you would like to say at this point.

Santangelo: Well, I don't think so. I mean, I hope I'm being an interesting subject for you.

Q: Oh, very. You certainly are. You certainly are. To me it's been tremendously interesting, it really has been. OK, thanks very much, Tony, and I guess we'll stop right here.

Santangelo: OK.

PART III

Making Meaning: Toward Understanding Tony Santangelo's Experienced Life Course

INTRODUCTION: RECOUNTER'S VOICE AND INTERPRETER'S VOICE

Clausen (1985, p. 11) has stated that "the meaning of any life is most fully apparent to the person leading that life." That this is an incomplete perspective can be seen if we recast the thought in this form: "The meaning of what a person says in an interview is most fully apparent to the person who is answering the interviewer's questions." In forms of qualitative interview other than life history, the interviewer seeks the interviewee's own words. These are essential to understanding the interviewee's point of view, the aspects of a topic that he attends to, the terms and assumptions with which he frames them, the quality of attention that he gives or doesn't give to a range of possible elements of the topic, and, indeed, the extent to which the interviewee grasps the meaning of what he is saying. But few researchers assume that the interviewee's own statements exhaust all the essential meaning in them or even that the meaning of the responses is most fully apparent to the interviewee. And this is for good reason. The researcher has a purpose in conducting the interview, a goal for presenting questions to which answers are being sought. The topic of the interview is problematic for the researcher in ways which it is not likely to be for the interviewee. This is as true for life history interviews as for any other.

The recounter's voice is essential. The account he provides is his currently available inventory and integration of what is significant in his life, what is meaningful. But the researcher asks meaningful questions about this material that derive from his research perspective. Sometimes life histories are published to document a social situation [Susan Tucker (1988), *Telling Memories Among Southern Women: Domestic Workers and Their Employers in the Segregated South*; Oscar Lewis, *The Children of Sanchez* and his Cuban life histories; Mark Traugott's (1993) *The French Worker: Autobiographies from the Early Industrial Era*]. My purpose in obtaining, presenting, and interpreting this life history of Tony Santangelo is to add to the study of the life course, to expand the boundary of that enterprise to incorporate the study of the experienced life course. I come to the work with a focus on human development, and I approach it not with a view to constructing a universal series of stages (such as Erikson 1950 or Levinson et al. 1978). Rather I want to examine the life history to understand how a person constructs his life—how he understands himself and others in his social participation, how he makes decisions, how he construes the opportunities and obstacles in his life, how he periodizes his own life, how the various periods of his life are connected, if they are.

I began this study with the two puzzles that I discussed in Part I. To try to solve those puzzles I developed a life history interview guide to use with Tony and the other men I interviewed and which is reproduced in the Appendix. But when I began to study Tony's life history, I did not have in mind any particular categories for analysis. The categories that organize the presentation in Part III arose in the course of reading and rereading the life history many times. As I did so, elements of the narrative prompted me to consider concepts that I know and that I thought would be helpful in understanding Tony's experienced life course. For example, I know the social psychological concept "significant other," and I reviewed some literature on that topic, which I cite. But I asked some questions that I did not find answered in the literature. I want to know who are the significant others in a person's life and what are the events and processes through which they gain significance. I want to try to understand what kind of a self emerges from a life: Can I find ways in which it changed? Can I find ways in which some continuity of the self persists through changing circumstance? How do significant others influence self, change, and continuity? By looking at the entire complement of significant others whom Tony discusses in his life history narrative and the various ways in which they are significant, I believe that I have used an established concept in a new way that illuminates the experienced life course.

Established concepts were not always available to build on. As I considered Tony's life history in the light of the Freud-Mead puzzle—that is, the determinism-emergence antinomy that I set forth in Part I—I did not find a ready key to that puzzle. Neither pure determinism nor pure emergence seemed suitably descriptive or explanatory. There was more connection between Tony's adult life and his childhood than Mead's emergence (or Blumer's version of it) would acknowledge, but there was less determination of adult experience by childhood experience than Freud would have argued for. The key came from comparing how Tony Santangelo and Frank Schmidt began their life history narratives (Handel 1994) and comprehending these as interpretive acts. That led to the realization that adults are connected to their childhoods by the way they conceive of their beginnings, and this led to the concept of "sense of origin" (Handel 1994). With that conceptual foundation, as I further studied Tony's life history, I was able to add concepts that captured his interpretation of later experiences—sense of upbringing, perspective on childhood, sense of development. These four concepts, together with the concept of experienced passages of time, provide a basic framework for a hermeneutic understanding of the life course, an understanding of the life course as a person has experienced and reports his life in a narrative life history. These concepts, as well as the other concepts and categories utilized in Part III of the study, help to clarify the experienced life course as a significant form of the life course, different from such other forms of the life course as the expectable life course (Clausen 1986), the institutionalized life course (Kohli 1986a; Meyer 1986), the life course as shaped by the political state (Mayer and Müller 1986), and various others.

Whatever understanding I or any other reader of Tony Santangelo's life history comes to will not be identical to his understanding of himself and his life, although in some aspects there may be considerable overlap. There are two main reasons for the difference. As a researcher (1) I try to recognize implicit meanings and make them explicit; and (2) I reframe both implicit and explicit meanings by considering them in terms of categories and questions that are important for efforts to arrive at understandings of the life course and human development. I try to understand the meanings by which Tony Santangelo lives his life but I am likely to express them in ways that he cannot because of the background that I bring to the task and the questions I am addressing. I now turn to the task.

SENSE OF ORIGIN

That most people can remember little or nothing from the first few years of their lives has probably long been common knowledge, but Sigmund Freud gave this phenomenon a name and an explanation. His explanation has been challenged and made problematic by others, but his label is still serviceable as a shorthand for complex phenomena. His term for the inability of people to remember events of their earliest years is infantile amnesia or childhood amnesia. Although there is variation in the ages at which people claim the first memory of their lives, no person can give a credible account, based on his own recollection, of the first year or two or three of his life.

Nevertheless, when I asked Tony Santangelo to tell me the story of his life I asked him to "begin at the beginning and tell me as much as you remember." The beginning of his life history cannot in any literal sense coincide with the beginning of his life and the actual events of the first months and years. Still, he had a sense of how to begin. Knowing one's date of birth is culturally prescribed knowledge in American and many other societies. So, too, is place of birth. But cultural prescriptions are not rigid, and particularly in the first-time situation of telling a life story, culturally prescribed knowledge must be sorted and selected, assembled, and constructed individually in a narrative in the novel situation.

The situation is one of asymmetrical dialogue: an interviewer asking brief questions and seeking extended answers. From George Herbert Mead's (1934) analysis of the self we understand that a participant in an interactive dialogue is first engaged in an internal dialogue immediately prior to every interactive contribution. The self can be understood as a two-phase process consisting of an "I" phase and a "Me" phase. Before a person can say something to another person he must first tell it to himself in an internal dialogue of the I and the Me. This process is ordinarily so swift that it occurs below the level of consciousness. We become aware of it when in difficulty. If Tony had said out loud, "Let's see, how should I begin?" he would have opened a window for us to see and hear the inner dialogue get started. Perhaps Tony did silently begin this way. We don't know. What is essential in the present context is that the way in which Tony begins his life history is not simply a ritual enactment of a culturally prescribed litany. It is an individually constructed statement of how his life began, a statement fashioned out of cultural materials but shaped by his own experience. It contrasts with other life history beginnings (Handel 1994). Each person telling his life history has some power of agency in situating his life in his society and in utilizing the culture he has acquired.

While the beginning of Tony's life history does not recount the first events of his life, except for reporting the date of his birth (obviously based on information obtained much later from others), it does communicate a particular *sense of origin*, a sense of how his life began. What he communicates is a sense of being rooted in a particular parish in a particular community, a person with a longstanding tie to a place and an institution, a tie that was initiated by parents whose origins were elsewhere. Their origins give him an uncertainly apprehended ethnic identity as "more or less of an Italian American." That he is more certain of his rootedness in his community is suggested by his assertion that "everybody calls me Tony," as well as by his recounting of his parents', his own, and his children's participation in the parish. The identity is clinched in his statement " . . . so you can see I'm really a native Yorkville man." His sense of origin conveys his subjectively meaningful beginning and the identity it gave him.

SENSE OF UPBRINGING

The earliest events of a person's life are not available to his later memory because memory has not developed sufficiently for them to be remembered (Schachtel 1959; Wexler and Sweeney 1988; Ross 1991). One leading explanation is that the young child does not yet have the categories necessary for remembering events. Those categories are acquired as language is acquired and words are attached to events and experiences. But even after categories develop, human memory does not retain every experience. Some experiences may be retained in their particularity and can be retrieved at a later age. Others blend into categories in a process that Schutz has called "typification." As phrased by his interpreters, Peter Berger and Thomas Luckmann (1967),

> . . . while it is comparatively difficult to impose rigid patterns on face-to-face interaction, even it is patterned from the beginning if it takes place within the routines of everyday life. . . . The reality of everyday life contains typificatory schemes in terms of which others are apprehended and dealt with in face-to-face encounters. (pp. 30–31)

Just as interactions with others may be organized as typifications, so also may these be organized in a larger cognitive scheme. An adult cannot remember every childhood conversation or encounter with parents and perhaps can remember no particular conversation or encounter at all. But from all of them he can distill a sense of how he was raised, *a sense of upbringing*.

Tony Santangelo conveys a sense of having had a protected upbringing. But he also identifies an overprotected aspect and an underprotected aspect. He says that he was a "Mama's boy," implying that he was held too close and was overprotected by her. But he also felt afraid of his father, not adequately protected by him and from him, even though he felt his father loved him. He does not report being beaten by his father, but he is vivid in his remembered apprehension of his father's drunken behavior. Yet the drinking had at least a double meaning, if not a triple or quadruple meaning for Tony. When drunk, Tony's father was aggressive toward Tony's mother and evoked fear in his son. But he also became better natured and more liberal toward Tony, an easier touch for money than when he wasn't drinking. These two appear to be meanings constructed contemporarily, to which Tony adds a retrospective interpretation: Perhaps the opportunity to drink was what kept his father working as a bartender. And he provides a fourth meaning, probably also retrospective rather than contemporary: If his father had not spent so much money on drinking, the family could have afforded more comforts than it had.

Tony's sense of upbringing highlights, perhaps more clearly than most other aspects of the experienced life course communicated in his life history, the blending of early and retrospective interpretation. When he says that the family might have enjoyed more comforts if his father had not spent so much on drinking, he is very likely assigning a meaning to three aspects of his childhood experience (father's employment, father's drinking, and family's material deprivation) from a later, adult perspective. It is less likely, though not impossible, that he constructed such a meaning when he was 8 or 9 years old. When he says that his father was verbally abusive to his mother, and also that his mother taught him to fear his father, it is more likely that he is reporting experiences and emotions that he remembers he experienced as a child.

PERSPECTIVE ON CHILDHOOD

One of the enduring issues in human development is the significance of early experience for later life. This is a complex issue; its full complexity cannot be explored here, but a schematic representation of it is useful. The issue was set by Freud, who argued that basic character is formed by the age of six or so and that actions in later life are essentially symbolic reenactments of the kinds of experiences that led to the establishment of character. The statement by Philip Rieff quoted in Part I provides a compact summary of Freud's view of this issue. The scholars of life-span development, beginning with Erikson (1950), argue that a person develops in later life in ways that make him different from what he was like in childhood. A person has experiences that he could not have had as a child, and these later experiences can and do have a formative effect on the person and on his ongoing life course. Adult life is therefore not simply a symbolic repetition of childhood. This type of conclusion, shared by others, sometimes incorporates an assumption that since adult life is not a repetition of childhood it follows that childhood experience does not influence that of adult life. This assumption is unnecessarily reductive. Repetition or similarity is not the only indicator of influence.

When we approach this issue from the standpoint of the experienced life course, we must begin with the implication that experiences are interpreted as they occur. Those initial interpretations, cognitive and emotional, may be remembered as specific occasions, but often they may be aggregated and blended into typifications. As the person moves out of childhood toward greater independence, he must choose a path that necessarily reflects an interpretation of childhood. That is, he must adopt a stance toward or perspective on his typified childhood experience as a guide to the kinds of experience he will seek in departing from childhood.

As a preliminary way of studying this issue, I want to propose that there are four main ways in which a person can interpret his childhood. One way is to accept the experiences of childhood as either good or necessary or both. Such an interpretation will likely result in a life course in which the person seeks experiences that are similar to, harmonious with, or elaborations of those of childhood. Such an interpretation will likely result in a life course that is essentially *elaborative* of childhood experience. But a person can interpret his childhood experience as bad, undesirable, harmful, unwanted, a summation of what should not have been and should not be. This perspective leads to a search for a life course that is *dissociative* from childhood. Childhood is typified as something to discard in its entirety. The person tries to build a life that bears no resemblance to the experiences of childhood. A third perspective or interpretive stance regards childhood experience as having been at least satisfactory in many aspects but to have been blotted, disfigured by some major flaw, some damage, something that should never have been. This perspective leads to a life course that is *restitutive*, a life course in which the person attempts fundamental repair of major childhood injury. Finally, the fourth possibility requires separate terms for the stance toward childhood and the subsequent life course. The stance is one that does not directly form the basis for the subsequent life course. Rather, childhood experience can be interpreted as benign but outgrown, leading to a life course that is *innovative*, one that seeks experiences quite different from those of childhood—thus not elaborative, but also not based on repudiation or repair, thus neither dissociative nor restitutive.

These four interpretive stances toward or perspectives on childhood (and the four prospective types of life course) have been presented as alternatives, but they are best regarded as ideal types. Actual lives may be blends. Further, it should not be assumed that they are necessarily lifelong. A person living an elaborative life course may switch to a dissociative one; a switch from dissociative to elaborative can also occur. An elaborative life course can become an innovative one.

How can we characterize Tony Santangelo's life from the vantage point of perspective on childhood? His life course gives little indication of a dissociative direction. It appears to be primarily elaborative, but with a restitutive element. What is the documentation?

An initial indication is provided by his sense of origin. His account of the beginning of his life presents him as a man who has maintained in adulthood his participation in the parish in which he was raised, as well as one who continues to reside in the neighborhood in which he spent his childhood. His brief move to the Bronx was not reflective of a wish to lead a different life in a different neighborhood but a temporary convenience that proved not satisfying. Further, although his military service took him to other regions of the United States and to Japan, these experiences did not awaken in him a desire to leave the familiar for pursuit of a different life. Nor did he take advantage of the educational benefits of the GI Bill of Rights to which he was entitled.

A disposition to rely upon parental advice is more suggestive of an elaborative stance than a dissociative, restitutive, or innovative one. Tony reports on more than one occasion that he turned to his father for advice and assistance in getting a job, notwithstanding the fact that he rejected his father's advice the first time it was offered, which was before it had been asked for.

Perhaps an equally profound indicator of an elaborative stance is Tony's understanding of how to function as a man in the world of work. He refers to his bartender father visiting other bars and tipping the bartenders in them, part of a mutual round robin of such visits, as a way of building goodwill.

When he talks about his own stopping off after work to have drinks with fellow construction workers, he explains his actions as building goodwill, necessary to maintain a place in the the uncertain job assignment world of construction. His father had a gift for meeting and speaking with people. Tony says he is always meeting new people and there are very few he doesn't get along with.

But his father's drinking inflicted pain on him in childhood, and he makes an effort to live in a way that repairs some damage, that is weakly restitutive. He reports that, like his father, he is a heavy drinker, but he further reports knowing when to stop and becoming quiet or getting sick rather than becoming abusive. And so his drinking is both part of an elaborative life course and a restitutive element within it. He drinks to build goodwill, just as he learned his father did in his job, but he does not become abusive as a consequence of drinking, and in this way tries to halt the damage he experienced in childhood.

The concept of perspective on childhood is useful for providing an overview of life course direction. It is not, however, a concept to which the experienced life course can be reduced. What I am asserting here is that every person must in some way interpret his childhood experience and must in some way incorporate those interpretations into the construction of his life course. Trying to understand the recounter's interpretations provides the social scientist with one vantage point, but only one, for understanding the recounter's experienced life course.

SENSE OF DEVELOPMENT

While Tony's life course has proceeded largely on the basis of an elaborative perspective on his childhood, this does not mean that he has merely grown older doing the same kinds of things he experienced in childhood. On the contrary, Tony has a *sense of development*. He has a sense of himself as someone who has made perceptive observations and learned important lessons, as a result of which he developed into a person of moderately broad understanding. Although he feels economically frustrated and believes he did not manage his work life in a way that would bring him the financial rewards some of his contemporaries have gained, he considers himself more than commonly insightful and knowledgeable about people. He credits himself with developing "street smarts" in childhood and adolescence and with utilizing his years of work as a bartender as an opportunity to gain insight into human nature. His army experience at military bases in the Deep South and in Japan enlarged his view of the world and consequently his view of himself as someone who had a larger view than before. While Tony considers himself economically stuck at an unsatisfying level of comfort and security, he does not consider himself experientially narrow. He does not see himself as someone who has gotten older in place but as someone who has grown, even while cherishing a familiar life.

EXPERIENCING THE PASSAGE OF TIME

A person's life course is a swath of time delimited by two biological end points, birth and death. Societies tend to recognize divisions of that unit based on interpretations of physiological capacity and social participation, so that some concept of age grading is probably found in all of them. Some students of the life course focus their work on identifying the emergence of life course subunits in the stream of social change. Thus, in one of the best known of such endeavors, Philippe Aries (1962) identified the emergence of childhood as a socially recognized phase of the life course, differentiated from a previously recognized period of infancy that lasted until age seven. (See also William Kessen 1981.) Adolescence has been described as a unit that emerged in the wake of the Industrial Revolution (Musgrove 1964). During the 1970s Kenneth Keniston and John Gillis independently suggested that changes in social participation were leading to a new grouping of years into a subunit called "youth," which was perhaps displacing adolescence (Gillis 1974; Keniston 1970). More recently, because of increased life expectancy, old age has been subdivided into two categories, leading to a distinction between "the young old" and "the old old." As such age categories become socially recognized and accepted, they become units of the expected life course.

When we shift our focus from the expected life course to the experienced life course we address a different problem. The socially standardized subunits of the life course that are recognized in a society at any given time provide a framework discernable in a life history, but the narration reveals personally experienced variations and idiosyncratic events that contribute to the recounter's sense that he is living a personally distinctive life, as well as a life that is immersed in society.

If we look at Tony Santangelo's life history from the point of view of units of time, we can see that he talks about time in a variety of ways. These do not lend themselves to a single systematic schema, so it is useful rather to work inductively to try to grasp how he relates to the temporal passage of his life.

One distinction that suggests itself early on is between *dismissed time* and *salient time*. Dismissed time is exemplified in his statement "I did eight years of grammar school." Here are eight years with no elaboration of narrative. He gives no recall of a teacher, of a learning experience, of a school friendship, or any other kind of experience. His account of his high school years is similar: " . . . Let's see, after I graduated, I went to Benjamin Franklin High School. I did two and a half years up there." In contrast to these unelaborated accounts is his description of one year, the year he got out of the army. He explains why he chose not to go to work at age 20 after leaving the army. The government was paying $20 per week for up to one year to veterans who were unemployed. And he explains that "I guess at that age . . . I thought the world owed me a living," and he went with his friends to Rockaway, a popular beach in New York. Dismissed time, then, is time spent in activity that is perceived as irrelevant to the self ("I started to get away from schoolwork . . . I guess I wasn't the type for it.") Salient time is time that is personally meaningful, time that has a recognizable relationship to self-awareness, self-conception, self-evaluation. Dismissed time is unimportant to the life course as experienced and recalled in a life history; salient time is meaningful time.

A second way in which the time of an experienced life course is distinguished is between *routine periods* and *remarkable events*. Tony's school years and the year that he believed the world owed him a living both have a routine character. They are both presented as lengthy periods, each having a stable character. Tony "did" the school years; he "used to go to Rockaway" as long as the $20 per week lasted. In contrast are remarkable events that are emotionally significant. Getting a first refrigerator and a first telephone as late as 1950, getting steam heat as late as 1959, being robbed in 1966, and his brother's heart attacks stand out in his mind as punctuating moments. Remarkable events, whether desired—as the (belated) acquisition of refrigerator, telephone, and steam heat—or undesired and unwelcome—as the robbery and the heart attacks—enlarge experience beyond its previously known limits. Remarkable events need to be distinguished from turning points because their occurrence does not have an impact that is experienced as a change in life direction or as a change in the self. They endure as recollected events but not as guides to subsequent social participation and action. They are memorable for the surprises they delivered but not otherwise persistently consequential. Turning points, in contrast, are self-recognized as resulting in changed participation, action, self-knowledge and/or self-evaluation.

Tony's experienced life course includes another kind of time, time that he would rather not think about. This consists of "the nights that my father came home drunk and arguing with my mother over petty things as I was laying in bed. . . . I believe I was scarred with the arguments of my mother and father." These arguments occurred at a particular time and formed a recurrent pattern. Tony's assessment of their impact on him indicates that he experienced those times lying in bed as a distinctive category in the passage of time. They constitute *damaging time*, time in which he experienced recurrent injury and pain.

Finally, we take note of *turning points*, a category of time that has been discussed by earlier scholars and is widely used as a folk concept. Hughes (1958) talked of turning points as important transitions in careers. Strauss (1959) talked of turning points in terms of significant changes of self, which is how the concept is understood and used today. It is distinguished from transition rather than being synonymous. The concept of transitions is central to much recent work on the life course, and it refers to the movement from one institutionally recognized status to another—such as getting married, getting a first job, having a first child (Elder, Modell, and Parke 1993, p. 4). Transitions and turning points do not necessarily coincide either in chronology or in significance for the life course.

Life course transitions in the sense of changes in institutionally established statuses are clearly reported in Tony Santangelo's life history, and these are somewhat important for his experienced life course. By his own account, however, the most important turning point in his life is not one laid out on an institutionalized pathway. Rather, it is being invited by a friend across the street, Charlie Rooney, to play baseball with the St. Ignatius team. Tony reports this as the most significant turning point in his life, one that enabled him to escape the probabilities of delinquency and crime that he saw awaiting him in his own neighborhood and that enabled him to move into an ordered but exciting world of organized sports. The invitation no doubt came because of his established reputation as a good ballplayer, but it was not predictable. This invitation was for Tony an illumination of lasting consequence and in more than one way. He acquired his fullest, if not his first, experiential understanding of wealth and status differences in Yorkville. He was introduced to money transactions larger than any he had known, and the uniforms and equipment with which his team was outfitted lifted him to a higher standard. His account of how the social distance between himself and his teammates eventually cancelled their shared baseball skills is poignant:

> We had a real close relationship. These were the fellows from St. Ignatius I'm talking about, by the way. But they all went on to take aptitude tests for jobs. I didn't. . . . I never figured I was a smart kid. I knew these kids were always smarter than me, from St. Ignatius. Maybe it was the education they had. I don't know. They took time out. I didn't really take time out. I wasn't much for opening a book after I got out of grammar school.

There is no doubt that Tony feels the social distance between himself and his teammates. As he says, he used to think about it a lot. He attributes that distance to his own lack of interest in schooling, which he accepts as unchangeably self-defining and therefore as setting him unalterably on a different trajectory from theirs. Yet, he clearly feels himself their equal on the ball field. His membership on that team yields one of the transcendent remarkable moments of his life, winning the New York championship in the Catholic Youth League and representing the state in the Little World Series in Battle Creek, Michigan, in 1949. His reputation as a ballplayer endures, and years later he is asked by Father Durney to coach in his home parish. He reports the priest asking him, "Tony, what's the matter? You've played ball all your life. Don't you think you could pass something on to the kids in this neighborhood who need it, and they're looking for a leader?"

Tony's response is an example of what Norman Denzin has called "an epiphany." Denzin (1989, p. 70) writes: "Epiphanies are interactional moments and experiences which leave marks on people's lives. . . . They alter the fundamental meaning structures in a person's life." Tony's report of his response to Father Durney is surely an instance: "And he made me feel like, gee, I never considered myself like an instructor or anything like that who could pass anything on to kids, you know. And I took time out. I told my wife about it. And it meant being away from the house more, too, getting up early on a Saturday, going over at 8 in the morning with kids, because that was the time we had the field, playing baseball with them, teaching them the fundamentals of the game, the sportsmanlike conduct and everything like that. I did the baseball teams for him, for the parish, and then in the winter I did the hockey teams, and that was like traveling all over the city to play the different games and sports. It cut into my time, but I enjoyed it, and I know I was helping him out, too, and he really appreciated it. He told me what a job I was doing and everything like that, and it was good to hear."

Father Durney's invitation to teach sports gave Tony a new view of himself. A boy who didn't like school, he never imagined himself an instructor, but that is what he became and committed himself to on Saturday mornings. This non-scheduled status passage (Glaser and Strauss 1971, pp. 60–61) changed Tony's experienced life course, even as it represented a revived continuity with the early aspiring self that brought him to St. Ignatius, to Battle Creek, and to tryouts with three major league baseball teams. He was once again "a neighborhood somebody."

Marriage is one of the widely recognized transitions in the life course. In Tony's life, no event seems as obviously influenced by his immediate social circle as his getting married. He reports that seven or eight in his group of friends "got wiped out that year." Tony's choice of words can be understood as a wry, mordant, colloquial version of Clausen's formal statement: "The transition from single to married status is certainly one of the most fateful changes of status to occur during the whole life course" (Clausen 1985, p. 134).

Yet this public change of Tony's status was not matched by a corresponding experiential change. Asked whether he found it hard to give up his single life, Tony replies that "My wife claims I never gave it up," and goes on to describe how he often delays going home for dinner at an expected hour in order to have a drink with someone he meets on the street after work. Tony does not directly acknowledge that these actions are those of a single man rather than a married one. Instead, he attributes the view to his wife, while acknowledging that he acts as she claims he does and while also professing that she accepts his actions, despite being "annoyed." What seems clear is that for Tony there is something of a disjunction between marriage as a transition in his life course and as a turning point in his experienced life course. He continues the pattern of after-work sociability with peers that he enjoyed as a single man, a pattern he wants to regard as compatible with marriage, while his wife defines it as a failure to complete the transition to marriage.

Phases

Academic disciplines such as psychology and sociology assume (for contemporary society) a more or less standard division of the life course into periods of infancy, childhood, adolescence, adulthood, and old age. This division of the life course is also part of the widespread popular stock of knowledge that is taken for granted. Although there are various refinements adduced in particular circumstances, this general framework is reflected in institutional divisions, such as schools, youth organizations, and other institutions that have age criteria or expectations for entry. These categories enter into the experienced life course, but they do not necessarily constitute its most meaningful divisions.

Tony Santangelo has experienced some clearly demarcated phases, while other years of his life do not seem to constitute such clear units of time. The phases are of varying length; furthermore, the same chronological years can sometimes be part of more than one phase. The clearest example of the latter is the year after he got out of the army, which in his mind is a distinctive period when he "thought the world owed me a living." That same year, however, is also part of a phase of at least three years when he was a member of the St. Ignatius parish baseball team. Somewhat similarly, his childhood is not a unitary block of time; nor is it divided simply by chronology. While his school years are a single phase—"I did eight years of grammar school"—some of those same years are remembered as years when he was his mother's movie-going companion. The point to be emphasized here is that it is an oversimplification to regard the experience of time as entirely socially structured, if by that term is meant the socially standardized divisions of time. Tony's experience of a movie-going companionship phase with his mother, is of course, socially constructed, but it is constructed at a primary-group level. Obviously, it is based on the cultural institution of movie theaters; however, the Santangelo family's manner of participation in that institution was not standardized but created within the family. It was created out of diverse components, particularly free passes which could only be used on week nights, Tony's father's nighttime job which prevented him from using them, and Tony's mother's wish to make use of them. The result is a phase of his life that he remembers as one in which he was his mother's steady companion.

THE SIGNIFICANCE OF SIGNIFICANT OTHERS

Every man must make his own life, but he does not make it alone. He makes it in interaction with many others. Robert Perinbanayagam notes that "all sociologists . . . accord a sense of importance to the concept of the other in their sociologies" (1975, p. 500). He expresses that importance generically as follows: "[T]he 'other' forms the self as the self formulates the 'other.' In all situations of social life, the 'other' is manifest, concretely or abstractly. And as the 'other' manifests itself, its character and content become causally significant to the emergence of the self and *its* nature and content" (p. 503).

But situations, and therefore others, are not all equally consequential. The others who are influential in a person's life are *significant others*. Further, as Morris Rosenberg observes, "not all significant others are equally significant" (Rosenberg 1973, p. 830). Rosenberg, and, in a more diffuse way before him, Hughes (1962) opened up the general question of the different kinds of significance that significant others can have, but no one has previously sought to examine the question in the context of an experienced life course. Who are the significant others in Tony Santangelo's experienced life course, and what are the different ways in which they are significant?

Answering this question by examining a life history entails a departure from the methodology of Mead and Rosenberg. Mead stated, "We are more or less unconsciously seeing ourselves as others see us" (1934, p. 68). Rosenberg developed and refined Mead's proposition: "We are more or less unconsciously seeing ourselves as we think others *who are important to us and whose opinion we trust see us*" (Rosenberg 1973, p. 857; italics in original). It is not clear to me why Mead and Rosenberg should have restricted the influence of significant others to unconscious influence, as though a person could not be aware of having been influenced by a significant other. The restriction seems unwarranted. Tony Santangelo tells us quite clearly about some of the significant others in his experienced life course, and we take these accounts seriously. It is, of course, also possibly the case that he may have been importantly influenced by people whom he does not mention and of whom he is not aware. Unconscious influences are not at all ruled out by insisting that conscious influences are also significant and that the recounter may be at least partially aware of how these significant others contributed meaningfully to his life.

Analytically, a distinction must be drawn between unspoken and unconscious influences. Tony volunteers nothing about his teachers and school classmates (a matter on which, in hindsight, I should have probed). Thus we cannot tell in what ways, if any, his experiences with them influenced him to quit high school before graduation. When Tony tells us that he did not consider himself as smart as the St. Ignatius teammates he played baseball with in his late teens and early twenties, was that because he was intimidated by their superior wealth and social standing? Or had his earlier school experiences with teachers and high school classmates already shaped his self-concept as a not-so-smart student? Had his teachers driven him from school by their negative evaluations or by the insufficiency of their efforts to keep him involved in school? Tony himself reports that he might have been influenced by an out-of-school crowd that he hung out with.

S. M. Miller and Frank Riessman (1968) argued that some high school dropouts should in fact be regarded as "pushouts." Pushouts are students who find school boring and confining, and their wish to get away from school is matched by the school's wish to be rid of them.

Is that what happened to Tony? He himself takes primary responsibility now for his decision to leave school. Perhaps if I had probed he would have recounted school experiences that would have made it possible to infer that teachers were either unconscious or even conscious influences on his decision to leave school. Regrettably, I did not probe sufficiently on this topic, and so it is not possible to decide whether teachers or classmates were such significant others for him that they impelled him from school and thereby weakened his lifelong employment options. A definitive affirmative answer, in the context of that missing inquiry, can now be given only if the issue is reframed in terms of political ideology, so that one declares that any student who quits high school before graduation is the victim of inadequate institutions and their inadequate agents, who must thereby be regarded as very significant others for the victim. From a public policy viewpoint, this is a meritorious frame, but in the present instance it is not phenomenologically appropriate. Tony does not define himself as a victim but as someone who should have listened to his parents' pleas to remain in school.

Although as a teenager Tony did not take his parents' advice to finish high school, it is evident that they were significant others in his life, and in several different ways. He says that his parents loved him. They gave him membership in a parish community which became the lifelong anchor for his life. His father's occupational practice of visiting other bartenders on his night off, which Tony interprets as building goodwill, became a model for his own drinking behavior, which he also interprets as building goodwill to stay afloat in his somewhat chancy occupation as construction worker. Knowing how to get along with others is for Tony a key to managing his life, and he sees his father as the person from whom he learned to appreciate the importance of "building goodwill."

Tony's father was significant in another important way. Tony describes himself as "selfish," a self-characterization whose meaning is not immediately apparent and one that puzzled me for a time. I now believe that this self-characterization can be understood as expressing a theme in his family, one that begins in his family of origin and continues in his family of procreation. "A family theme is a pattern of feelings, motives, fantasies, and conventionalized understandings grouped about some locus of concern which has a particular form in the personalities of the individual members.

The pattern comprises some fundamental view of reality and some way or ways of dealing with it. In the family theme are to be found the family's implicit direction, its notion of 'who we are' and 'what we do about it' " (Hess and Handel 1995, p. 11)

A major theme in Tony's family of origin is a conflict between self indulgence and responsibility. Tony's father was self-indulgent in his drinking, managed to stay sober enough to keep his job as a bartender in the restaurant established by Tony's grandfather but was not considered dependable enough to be given an ownership or managerial stake. Tony made some decisons in his life that can be considered as choosing self-indulgence over responsibility. Declining to apply for a job in the Department of Sanitation when he quit high school because it entailed working half a day on Saturday is possibly of this character, as is, more certainly, his decision to not seek work for a year after leaving the army because veterans were guaranteed fifty-two weeks of unemployment income. When Tony's wife complains that he often doesn't show up for dinner on time and that he never got over being single, her complaint can be seen as one about his self-indulgence and lack of responsibility toward her.

This theme can be seen not only in his relation to his father but to his mother as well. He tells us that as a child he was a "Mama's boy," and that his mother made few demands on him. He could come and go as he pleased. He sees this as a flaw in the way she raised him, and now takes a restitutive tack in struggling with his son to take some responsibility at home. The family theme is manifest also in the contrast that Tony draws between his brother and himself. He says that his brother does not know how to relax and worries about everything, whereas "my wife says all I do is relax." Tony recognizes that his wife sees him as self-indulgent, a characterization he does not disclaim, whereas he perceives his brother as a person who feels responsible for managing even very small matters. A family theme manifests itself differently in different family members; they are united by the issue, not by how each has dealt with it.

Tony reports material deprivation in childhood and also emotional scarring from his father's repeated quarreling with his mother. Yet he does not come across as a deeply embittered person, despite those early experiences and despite his contemporary envy of agemates who made what he now considers wiser occupational decisions. One fundamental reason is that his parents did give him his initial strengths, as well as enmeshing him in an enduring inner and interpersonal conflict of trying to balance self-indulgence with responsibility.

Tony's older brother is also a significant other in his life. He regards his brother as his idol, whose commitment to sports provided his own inspiration in that direction. And since Tony credits his passion for sports for saving him from a potentially antisocial life he acknowledges an enormous debt to his older brother. The inspiration he took from his brother was renewed by Charlie Rooney who played a decisive role in switching Tony to the track that brought him perhaps his deepest satisfaction in his early life, his participation as a member of the St. Ignatius baseball team. Their CYO championship is one of the major highlights of his life and contributed to his being offered tryouts with major league teams. The public reputation he gained received revival from Father Durney many years later when he defined Tony as someone who could teach sports to youngsters. And Tony knew himself to be the apple of his father's eye for his baseball prowess. Thus we gain a clear picture of how brother, father, streetmate, and priest served as complementary significant others in making possible one of the more significant parts of Tony's experienced life course. His sense of himself as a possible baseball player and his knowledge of himself as an accomplished player were shaped by contributions from these four significant others. In addition, Father Durney enlarged Tony's self concept by endowing him with a new identity built on the old—player into teacher.

Tony formed a relationship with his first girl friend, Helen, when he was 16, and he went with her for about three years. He reports that he was not interested in girls prior to that time because he was totally engrossed in sports. Helen entered his life through an intermediary, a girl who told him that Helen wanted "to go with him," an expression he says he did not initially understand. Helen had considerable meaning for him. He credits Helen with educating him about females, although their amorous activities did not go beyond "the usual—the petting bit.... But as for going to bed, no way, no way." That their relationship did not include sexual intercourse is not something he attributes to Helen's resistance but to his own understanding of himself and his social milieu.

Tony avers that sexual intercourse was not something talked about in his crowd, although at another point in the interviews he says that perhaps others did talk about it and engage in it, but he thinks he was, at that age, afraid to take the step. He contrasts sexual age norms of that time with those of today and indicates that teens begin sexual activity today at a much earlier age than then. While we cannot know how accurately he is able to report on what his peers were doing sexually, there is little doubt that he is saying that he was not ready for sexual intercourse during his first heterosexual relationship and that he became ready only after he had served in the army. Despite the long interval, he credits Helen with having contributed to his sexual development.

Sexuality does not seem, however, to have been a powerful motif in his life. He does not make even an indirect allusion to sexuality in explaining his attraction to the woman who became his wife. Rather, he emphasizes that "She was a very congenial person, very congenial. She made everything easy for me, conversation-wise. She liked what I liked in life. We were very compatible more or less." The qualification "more or less" suggests that there might have been initial incompatibilities that were put out of mind so that the marriage could go forward. (We have already noted in-compatibilities in the marriage.) Tony's marriage and the births of his children renew and reiterate his membership in his community. Considering everything that Tony has told us about his life, we sense that membership in his community may be more fulfilling than his marriage. Nonetheless, he makes it clear that his marriage and family have an important meaning for him: they saved him from a life of rootlessness and aimless drift. He conjures up the alternative that his life might have been without them, a life of solitariness devoted to chasing women. He is indebted to his wife for saving him from that kind of life. With the security that this anchorage affords him, he feels free to keep up his community contacts, even though it often makes him late for dinner and leaves his wife "annoyed."

Tony reports that his wife says that he treats all his friends alike. Despite Tony's own demurral—his insistence that Lou is his special friend—there is a powerful suggestion in the life history that the most individually significant others came earlier in his life and that he now feels more comfortable in the warm glow of a supportive group than in individual one-to-one relationships. This is not to say that his wife and children are not important to him. They are. One of his great current satisfactions is his son's successful sports participation in his high school teams. His wife and children give him important identities as husband and father, and they give structure and order to his life, but clearly less order than his wife thinks they should.

SOCIAL DOMAINS: EXPERIENCES OF PARTICIPATION

To identify the significant others in Tony's life is to identify those people whose influence he recognizes as having contributed centrally to the kind of life he has led. He recognizes that what he considers his lifelong selfishness originates with the way his parents dealt with him. His lifelong passion for sports originates in his idolization of his older brother, even though the age gap between them, as well as wartime circumstance, meant that his brother was not very accessible to him. Charlie Rooney—who played the role of switchman in getting Tony out of his neighborhood crowd and onto the St. Ignatius team—Father Durney, and his first girlfriend, Helen, were in their different ways important in defining major turning points in his life.

Significant others are crucial in a man's life, but they do not constitute the fullness of his social participation. If we want to understand the breadth of a man's life course, we need to review the breadth of his social participation, insofar as these various social domains are accessible to us in his life history.

Family Memberships

Tony Santangelo is a son, brother, nephew, cousin, husband, and father, and all of these roles and statuses have had some impact on his life. We have considered his relationships with his parents and brother, as well as with his wife and children, so that comment on them here will be brief, with an effort at minimal repetition.

His father was both a positive and a negative role model. He was well liked in the neighborhood and Tony, from childhood on, endeavored and succeeded in being well liked in the neighborhood. But Tony was also the pained and resentful eavesdropper on his father's quarrels with his mother, quarrels whose origin Tony unambiguously attributes to his father. These meanings of his relationships with his parents are quite clear. Other aspects are less clear. Tony says he was his mother's constant companion, yet considers that his brother was his mother's favorite while he was his father's favorite. Although he says that he spent a great deal of time with his mother, he does not communicate that he had a particularly warm relationship with her. It was evidently companionable. Tony shows nothing but respect for his mother, but he does not report that she was supportive or encouraging, apart from her once taking up his cause with the mother of a boy who bullied him. He relied repeatedly on his father to help him get jobs, even though he earlier turned down his father's urging to remain in school and his offer to help him get a job in the Department of Sanitation.

When Tony was dissatisfied with his job at Hotpoint, his father's brother offered him a job as waiter, then bartender, in the restaurant his grandfather had established. His work as bartender turned out to be the most satisfying employment he had had, the employment he talks about most fully and most enthusiastically. After this uncle died and left the restaurant to another uncle who also died, Tony's hopes for inheriting the business were dashed by the latter's daughters, who sold the business, leaving him out in the cold. It is not clear how long Tony had nurtured an aspiration to inherit the business, but this hope of keeping the family name going is the last vocational aspiration that he gives voice to. Although we cannot know for certain, it is possible that the father's undependability if not actually attributed to his son, may have cast a shadow over Tony's employment and kept him from participation in ownership.

School

Although it would have been desirable to inquire further into Tony's participation with teachers and schoolmates, he does tell us something that communicates a basic meaning of school for him. His comparison of himself with his St. Ignatius teammates is revealing when he says, "I never figured I was a smart kid. I knew these kids were always smarter than me, from St. Ignatius. Maybe it was the education they had. I don't know. They took time out. I didn't take time out. I wasn't much for opening a book after I got out of grammar school." The elliptical expression "take time out" is reasonably clear and revealing in its meaning. To read a book and to become educated through reading is to take time out either from what are the interesting things in life or, at the very least, from what are the ordinary activities of life. To read a book is to take time out from what one is doing or what one wants to do, a digression from one's real life. For whatever reason, school did not become a part of Tony's real life. It had no meaning for him. But in his mid-forties he understands school and schooling in a different way, as a prerequisite to desirable employment. He compares himself with agemates who were able to make school a meaningful part of their lives and who can retire at his same age, while he has to struggle to earn a satisfactory living. Utilizing his own experience retrospectively and with a changed current and prospective assigned meaning to schooling, he threatens his son with punishment—"I told him if his marks go down I'll burn his hockey sticks"—if he does not earn adequate marks in school. He says the threat is effective. And yet, what does Tony mean as he continues: "But I have to get on him a little more with his studies. He hates to take time out. I imagine it's his age. He's just running around like, enjoying life. I wish I was his age today." Does Tony wish he were once again free to run around and enjoy life, or does he mean that if he were his son's age today he would use his adult wisdom to have a wiser adolescence? Both these meanings, contradictory though they are, very likely coexist.

Peer Groups: Friendship and Sociability

When he introduced the concept of primary groups, Charles Horton Cooley (1909) defined them as characterized by face-to-face association and cooperation. He considered them "fundamental in forming the social nature and ideals of the individual" (1909, p. 23). The most important primary groups were, he said, the family, the play group of children, and the neighborhood group of elders. Edward Shils (1951) thought that "small size and physical proximity (face-to-face relations) . . . [are] conditions affecting the formation of primary groups" (1951, p. 44) rather than their basic characteristics. What was basic in his view was "a high degree of solidarity, informality in the code of rules which regulates the behavior of its members, and autonomy in the creation of these rules. The solidarity involves close identification of the members with one another and with any symbols of the group which might have grown up" (Shils 1951, p. 44).

While suggesting that the concept of primary group should be considered a variable rather than a fixed category, Dexter Dunphy (1972) joined Cooley in considering primary groups fundamental in fashioning human nature or personality and joined Shils in identifying their basic criteria, as well as adding to them. He writes: "A group is primary insofar as it is based on and sustains spontaneous participation, particularly emotional involvement and expression. It also provides intrinsic personal satisfaction, that is, personal relationships in the primary group are considered valuable in themselves and not only as means to other ends" (Dunphy 1972, p. 5).

Tony Santangelo is highly conscious of how his participation in the play group—or peer group as it is now more commonly called—of childhood contributed to making him the kind of person he considers himself to be. In his childhood peer group he was always the youngest member, and he judges that there was about a three-year age gap between him and most of the others. This situation had two consequences. First, he was vulnerable to being bullied. He says that he wasn't much of a fighter. The older boys would protect him from bullying and he became, as he says, a mascot or pet for the group. He understood that his membership in the group was sustained by the fact that even at a young age he was an exceptionally good baseball player, better than some of those older. The second important consequence was that growing up from early on with older boys gave him knowledge that he values as useful throughout his life. "Most of the fellows I grew up with were older than me, and I think this helped me an awful lot growing up, because I didn't really have that babyish thing about me when I was small. I always hung out with fellows like three or four years older than me. I was always the youngest one in the crowd. I believe it gave me the smarts, the experience to handle different situations, you know." Tony thus believes that his membership in his childhood peer group provided him with an essential constituent of his being.

During adolescence his local peer group began to feel too rough for him. When he was about fourteen he was caught stealing a box of toothpicks from an A & P store, an item he neither needed nor wanted but stole to maintain his peer group membership by following the established pattern. His experience of being threatened by the store manager began to loosen his ties to this group. He began to play ball with St. Ignatius. "I would play ball for St. Ignatius, but I was still hanging out with my old group. Now, I was like between the two groups. The group that I used to hang out with, you know, that I was brought up with, wasn't much interested in sports. I found out that I had to go out of the neighborhood more or less to get into organized sports." But it wasn't until after he came back from army service that he separated from his original group and cast his lot with the St. Ignatius team wholeheartedly. He considered his original group too casual and unfocused in its approach to sports, as well as too involved in unlawful behavior.

As an adult, Tony is deeply committed to his peer group of workers in the construction trades who hang out at Joe Wagner's bar as their virtual clubhouse. He is sometimes in conflict with the group, as when some of the men want to embark on an escapade that he regards as dangerous. He also acknowledges ruefully having sometimes gone along on an escapade—going to Hoboken for clams—that was not dangerous but was unwelcome nonetheless. The avidity of his attachment to his group embroils him in repeated conflict with his wife, who cannot understand why he does not come home to relax after work, why he so often shows up late for dinner, and why he does not take her out more. He knows she is dissatisfied but he tries to minimize the extent of her dissatisfaction. His explanation to the interviewer that he builds goodwill with other construction workers and thus enhances his opportunities for construction work does not square very well with his statement that the men he drinks with are in construction trades other than his own and that he doesn't work with them. Nor does it fit with his statement that he obtains work through the union, not through informal contacts.

The meaning of this group for Tony comes through in the overall narrative of his life history, although it is a meaning he does not explicitly express: he is more comfortable with men than with women. More particularly, he is more gratified by the sociability in this peer group than by his wife's companionship. He portrays her as quite a controlled person, one who is easily offended by coarseness in movies and who feels she must clean the apartment thoroughly before friends can be allowed to come in for after-dinner snacks. Tony prefers a more casual, more relaxed atmosphere, but one that does not get wild, which he reports does happen sometimes in his group, at which point he leaves. His sociability preferences may explain why his wife wants to move from a Yorkville apartment to a house elsewhere, while Tony has no wish to do so.

Community Memberships

Tony's life history reveals a local community with a multifaceted organization, focused, from his point of view, on sports. He identifies three bases of organization, three different kinds of units to which loyalty and allegiance were given. The most important—that is, the most consequential in Tony's life—was the *parish* basis for baseball teams in the Catholic Youth Organization. Baseball elicited the greatest interest and evoked the most absorbing commitment of energy of almost any activity in his life. Tony regards his membership on the St. Ignatius parish team as the most significant shaping membership in his life.

A second sport in which he participated, hockey played on roller skates, was based on *residential blocks*. He was a member of the "89ths" and played teams based on other residential blocks. A league of such teams was organized by the city's Parks Department, and games were played in armories and other local arenas. Tony's skillful participation in this sport resulted in one memorable recognition that contributed to his local celebrity: through efforts of his hockey coach, his picture appeared on an inside cover of *TV Guide* magazine. This memorable experience still elicits from him a mixed reaction of pleasure and disbelief that he should have attained such prominence.

Finally, after he stopped playing baseball he took up softball and played in a league of teams sponsored by *neighborhood bars*. He indicates that he played for Joe Wagner's, the bar whose closing was featured in the *New York Times* story cited in Part I. It was while walking home from one of these games that he came alongside Catie and asked her to join him for a drink, the date which he fixes as the beginning of their relationship that led to marriage.

Here, then, is a highly organized local sports world for young non-college men, and young manhood avidly committed to sports. Parishes, residential blocks, and bars sponsored teams in one or another kind of league, providing men with meaningful memberships that brought out their neighbors as fans to cheer them on in their competitions. These local institutions, which gave them corporate identities, were knitted together in webs that reached across communities and joined local loyalty to the excitement of participation in a wider New York. Tony views this world as his salvation.

Work

A line of research extending back several decades to Robert Dubin (1956) and including such notable examples as the studies by Herbert Gans (1962) and Lillian Rubin (1976) has shown that work is not a central life interest of working-class men, that they think of it as little as possible but simply try to do their jobs. A later study showed that in some cases such men had, in their teens, nurtured realistic ambitions to enter work that was more skilled and moderately more prestigious than their fathers' lowly work but for various reasons they abandoned these ambitions (Handel 1991). The Dubin, Gans, and Rubin characterizations are applicable to part of Tony Santangelo's work life, but not to all of it, and there is more to be said than simply that he had to abandon his ambitions.

When Tony quit high school, he went to work as a delivery boy for a grocery store. He followed this with work on a loading dock for REA (Railway Express Agency), a package-shipping company. He then went into the army. After he was discharged, he did no work for a year, enjoying the unemployment benefits granted veterans, then took a job on the loading dock of the Coca-Cola Company, but was laid off after eight months. He resisted his father's urging to take a job with the City of New York Department of Sanitation, an offer his father was able to make because of political connections made at the bar-restaurant at which he worked. Instead, Tony became a laborer in the construction industry. During this period, he was playing ball in the CYO league and he had tryouts with three major league baseball teams. Had he been hired, he might well have felt committed to and enjoyed that work, but it did not happen; he had to abandon his ambition to be a professional baseball player. At the age of twenty-seven, after five years in construction work, he sought another job because construction employment was too irregular. For about two years he worked for the Hotpoint Division of General Electric Company, replacing burned-out units in refrigerators. He was unhappy in this work and accepted an offer from his uncle to work as a waiter and bartender in his restaurant.

In none of the jobs that he held until this point does he express any satisfaction whatsoever. He has little to say about them other than how much he was getting paid, what the hours were, how hard the work was. But this lack of involvement does not characterize his work as a bartender. On the contrary, he seems to have found considerable meaning in that work, and he is expansive about it. That satisfaction does not appear to have come from working in a family business; he does not volunteer much about his uncle as boss, although one can infer that their relationship was at least satisfactory since Tony progressed to night manager (which later made him a holdup target), a responsibility his father never had. This advancement made it not unreasonable for Tony to aspire to inherit ownership after his two owner-uncles died in succession.

But although Tony is disappointed that he did not inherit the bar and restaurant, he values his experience as a bartender. He believes it contributed greatly to his knowledge and understanding of the world. He says, "You get some education in a bar. You know, I got some experience. . . . I think I learned an awful lot about people. And how to handle people. You know, stuff like that. And how to cope with them, their troubles. Like you become a priest when you're a bartender. You become a father to the younger people. You listen to everybody's troubles. It's a known fact that a bartender just has an ear for troubles. The idea is to keep your mouth shut when you're a bartender. That's the idea, not to pass it on, not to pass it on. Just accept it, keep it inside you, and don't let on what's going on. That's what I believe."

Clearly, his years as a bartender were not just a job to Tony. This is not dismissed time or damaging time. It is salient time. These were years in which he believes he developed valuable insights into people and acquired a mature composure. He values what he learned and he values what he became in that time. His sense of pride in the way he constructed his role is evident. He has a sense of both significant work accomplished and personal experiential enrichment.

Ethnicity and Religion

Tony Santangelo is conscious of himself as an Italian-American. He classifies himself under this label near the very opening of his life history. And yet this identity seems to bring with it very little heritage and to have played very little part in his life course. He says that he comes from "Italian parents," but they were both born in New York City. It was their parents who were born in Italy and immigrated, thus making Tony's parents second generation and Tony third generation Italian American. Tony's parents spoke only a little Italian and not in their own home, only to their parents in theirs.

Tony accounts for the minimal cultural influence of his Italian background by a combination of personal and community characteristics, in addition to the minimal importance given it by his parents. He notes that his physical appearance differs from what he considers typically Italian: he describes himself as having chestnut hair and fair, light skin. More significantly, perhaps, he describes his peers, both in childhood and adulthood as being predominantly of other ethnic backgrounds, with a significant weighting of Irish. He further reports that, while there was a St. Patrick's Day Parade, there was not, during his childhood, a Columbus Day Parade. Indeed, the only explicit experience of "Italian-ness" that he reports in his life history is being called a "guinea" by an Irish American neighbor boy when he was seven or eight years old. This experience seems to have had little, if any, enduring significance in the way he subsequently constructed his life course. His relationship to his ethnic background exemplifies a general trend identified by Richard Alba that encompasses most, though not all, Italian Americans: "Italian Americans stand on the verge of the twilight of their ethnicity. 'Twilight' appears an accurate metaphor for a stage when ethnic differences remain visible but only faintly so, when ethnic forms can be perceived only in vague outline" (Alba 1985, p. 159).

Much more significant has been Tony's membership in the Catholic Church, an institution which he recognizes has given substantial structure to his life. Not only does he identify its importance early in his life history narration but he refers to church-related activities frequently thereafter. As already noted, the Catholic Youth Organization baseball league provided him with several years of enjoyable participation and with a peak experience of being on a state championship team. In later years he enjoyed dinners in his family's restaurant and going to athletic events with Father Durney. When Father Durney invited Tony to teach baseball to parish children, Tony's self-concept expanded significantly and his self-esteem increased. His ballplaying made him zestful, his teaching of baseball made him proud. Both brought him the community's esteem.

EXPERIENCING POVERTY

Tony Santangelo's entire life has been shadowed by poverty. Although he reports some brief periods when his family income was adequate, there is an almost persistent tone of economic deprivation. He has barely begun recounting his life history when he reports his belief that his father's drinking behavior reduced the family income when he was a child, resulting in a barely adequate standard of living. The family lived in a four-room tenement, and the living conditions generate a feeling of humiliation. As he details them, his recounting evokes not only a report of physical discomfort but of shame at having had to live below a standard that he believes his friends had. "You tell your friends you didn't have a refrigerator till 1950, they laugh at you. It's unbelievable. Especially a telephone in them days." The bathtub in the kitchen is another source of humiliation. This tone is relieved from time to time. When he went to work after enjoying the year on government unemployment pay of $20 a week ("just enough to get by on.... There was nothing going into the house") he takes some pride in telling how his earnings helped in "bringing a little luxury into the house, making it a little easier on my mother, which had worked hard all her life."

At the time of the interview he reports that he is making a reasonable amount of money but points out that as an ironworker in construction he doesn't get paid if it rains and he can't work. Yet even as he reports sufficient current income, he also says that he has virtually no money set aside for retirement and he foresees having to work for many years, even as he sees agemates retire.

Tony's experience of income inequality was dramatized when he joined the St. Ignatius baseball team and heard Father O'Shea make an appeal for funds from the pulpit so the team could have uniforms and good equipment. The speed with which the funds were collected from the congregation leads him to say "I had never seen anything like this in my life." It is interesting, that Tony is unable to come up with the expression "blank check." In trying to describe the financial freedom and the lavishnes of the total available he says Father O'Shea had "an unsigned check," then corrects himself and says "a signed check and all he had to do was fill in the amount of the figure for the equipment." He still feels remote from the world of large sums, especially large sums that can be put to discretionary use.

His continuing concern with having adequate funds shows up in an indirect way when he is discussing his friends and his wife's comments that he treats them all alike. When she presses him to say who his best friend is he names Lou Shanahan, and the evidence he gives for their friendship is that when they go out to dinner together with their wives he and Lou do not quibble over who pays for what. While this brief discourse on money and friendship may have more than one meaning, the most likely one seems to me to be this: Tony is saying that whatever one's struggle with personal finances, one should not let it spill out in a public friendship situation. Instead of "pinching the pennies right down," the honorable thing to do is to divide the dinner bill equally and to be magnanimous in paying the cab fare home without asking or expecting this expense to be shared. This practice is, to be sure, very common, but the meanings may not be the same in all cases. The interpretation that in Tony's case it involves suppressing personal concern with financial adequacy is based on his several mentions of this issue in his life and on the fact that the practice is the only evidence he gives for the specialness of his friendship with Lou, in contrast to other fel-

lows who pinch the pennies. He is telling us that he would like to rise above financial concerns and live on a plane of pure conviviality where money does not matter.

SYMBOLIC RESOURCES

Making a life requires resources. Resources are bestowed socially and genetically, but only as potentials. For these resources to be used in making a life the person on whom they were bestowed must take personal possession of them. A talent first recognized by others must become a personal possession, or it is not a resource. Thus, a neighbor of Tony Santangelo's, encouraged by a high school teacher to develop his talent for machine work and tool and die making, fails to accept the talent as his own to use in making his life, and becomes a letter carrier (Handel 1991, pp. 232–233.)

Resources are made available by the society through its language and other communication systems. They become personal through what Mead (1934) called the importation of the social process into the individual and thus become part of the inner dialogue of the self. This conceptualization can be taken a step further if we introduce Brim's (1976) concept of "theory of oneself." Brim writes:

> What humans learn during life are axioms, concepts, and hypotheses about themselves in relation to the world around them. We can think of the sense of self as a personal epistemology, similar to theories in science in its components and its operations, but dealing only with a specific person. The important thing to remember is that it is a self theory and that the sterile notion of the "self-concept" has stood in the way of further progress along this particular path. What we should say, more strictly, is that the self is a body of theory and that it is a segment of a human's whole theory of himself and the world around him.
>
> . . . Analysis of the meaning of an individual's sense of personal control over life also explores the theory of oneself, in that it deals with idiosyncratic personal theories of causality involving the person as an actor and the world outside as the object . . . (Brim 1976, p. 242)

Brim goes on to say that "we are dependent for our theories about ourselves on what is available in our culture" (p. 244). While this statement is unexceptionable, Brim goes astray, I believe, when he departs from all concept of agency in further stating that "The culture provides the interpretation of the individual event and the accumulated theory into which our own theories about ourselves must fit" (p. 244). The first part of this statement implies unmodified cultural determinism and leaves no room for the necessity of a person to construct his own interpretations in making his own life. If the culture provides the interpretation of the individual event, then presumably it would provide a completely formed theory of oneself as well. This view ignores, indeed contradicts, the earlier statement quoted above. Further, it ignores the implication that a theory of oneself is created by trial and error, by struggle to understand and come to terms with the events in one's life.

When we examine Tony Santangelo's account of his life, we can see many aspects of his theory of himself, and we can see that he has selectively drawn on cultural concepts and turned them into personal symbolic resources for making his life. He has interpreted aspects of his experience so as to make resources out of them.

Physique

We can never know why Tony Santangelo was not hired by any of the three major league baseball teams for which he tried out. As good a baseball player as he was, perhaps his batting, fielding, running, or throwing was not up to major league standards. But he does not at any time acknowledge such a skill limitation or deficiency. Rather, he explains one of the major disappointments in his life by referring to his slight physique. "But it was the same old story, 'We'll call you,' and I'm still waiting to hear from them. But I accepted it. Because I'm really not a big strapping fellow. I go about 5-7 and a half, about 160 pounds, and this was like, you know, 26 years ago, and I still hold to 160 pounds, so I try to keep in the best shape as I can." He does not say that he was told that his physique was what made him unacceptable. Indeed, he may have been told nothing other than what he says he was told, "We'll call you." The slight physique—the deficiently slight physique—becomes transformed into a resource, transformed into his own understandable and acceptable explanation for the great disappointment. In that way, his physique becomes a symbolic resource for getting on with his life. He has found in it something that helps him make sense of what has happened to him and why he had to move on to do something else with his life.

Age

Successive chronological ages have socially assigned meanings (Aries 1962; Gillis 1974). These assigned meanings play some part in every person's life, and they do in Tony's. At the time he recounted his life history to me he was ruefully comparing himself with agemates who had gone into such occupations as policeman and fireman, which assign retirement age and pension to a twenty-year period of service. But if there are some people who use age in their lives exclusively in terms of such structurally assigned meanings, that is not what Tony has done. As he interprets and finds meaning in his life, he has made age in childhood into a resource.

Tony Santangelo feels financially frustrated but interpersonally successful, at least in his peer world, if less so in his family. He prides himself on his ability to get along with people, and he prides himself on both his street smarts and his understanding of people. He sees these as accomplishments in living, and he gives a substantial amount of credit for them to his relative age in his childhood peer group. He says that he was always the youngest in his peer group and was treated as a kind of mascot. He was protected and received a kind of fostering by the group. He understands this age relationship to have given him security and knowledge emanating from his elder peers. He thus understands his age in childhood as a resource which he turned into meaningful accomplishment that continued in adulthood.

Sports Talent and Motivation

Tony's intense devotion to sports, as well as his talent in them, particularly baseball, are manifest in his life history and have been discussed in preceding contexts. They are mentioned here to take explicit notice that these, too, are symbolic resources, his most cherished ones. They are resources that he has used to symbolize himself and to construct his relationship with his community. They are resources he used to keep himself from a life in crime that he saw as an actual hazard.

Congeniality

Finally, in considering how Tony has made his way in life, we must note the importance he gives to his congeniality, his ability to get along with people. He interprets himself as a man who likes people, finds it easy to get along with them, and who has no enemies. He uses his congeniality to build goodwill.

THE SELF THROUGH TIME

To live as a human being is to give meaning to others, to events, to oneself. The capacity to give meaning is lodged in the self, which develops through communication and interaction with others. George Herbert Mead (1934, p. 140) states some defining characteristics:

> The self, as that which can be an object to itself, is essentially a social structure, and it arises in social experience. After a self has arisen, it in a certain sense provides for itself its social experiences, and so we can conceive of an absolutely solitary self. But it is impossible to conceive of a self arising outside of social experience. When it has arisen we can think of a person in solitary confinement for the rest of his life, but who still has himself as a companion, and is able to think and converse with himself as he had communicated with others.

At another point Mead notes that "we normally organize our memories upon the string of our self" (1934, p. 135).

In brief, the self arises out of social experience. It is a structure (and a process of inner dialogue) which makes use of language, thought, and emotion to interpret experience. It has two phases, which Mead called the "I" and the "Me"—an active experiencing phase and a phase that is the repository of experiences which can be remembered either in the form of specific events or in the form of typified categories of experience.

In the years since Mead, the concept of self has been developed further and elaborated. The activities of giving meaning to oneself have been conceptualized as self-evaluation or self-esteem and as self-concept. In this part of the analysis I want to try to elucidate these aspects of Tony Santangelo's self. Until now, I have attempted to give a systematic exposition of his social experience. I have also presented some aspects of his self-concept when I discussed his sense of origin, sense of upbringing, perspective on childhood, sense of development, and his symbolic resources. These were a part of my effort to understand the life course significance of how Tony had organized his memories on the string of his self. In the remainder of this section, I want to bring out additional aspects.

A couple of definitions are in order first. Morris Rosenberg defined the self-concept as "the totality of the individual's thoughts and feelings having reference to himself as an object" (Rosenberg 1979, p. 7). Viktor Gecas subsequently stated:

> An elementary but useful distinction is between the content of self-conceptions (e.g., identities), and self-evaluations (e.g., self-esteem). Identity focuses on the meanings comprising the self as an object, gives structure and content to self-concept, and anchors the self to social systems. Self-esteem deals with the evaluative and emotional dimensions of the self-concept. In experience, these two aspects of the self-concept are closely interrelated: Self-evaluations are typically based on substantive aspects of the self-concept, and identities typically have evaluative components. Within social psychology these two dimensions involve largely separate literatures (Gecas 1982, p. 4).

Despite the separate literatures, self-evaluations are, as Gecas states, intertwined with identities. The following subsections are given identity headings, but Tony's self-evaluations will be evident as well.

Gender Identity

The study of gender began as the study of women. It began at a time when most social scientists were male; masculinity was taken for granted as *the* basis for understanding the world, and femininity was considered something whose development needed to be studied. The efflorescence of women's studies that followed had, however, an initially unanticipated consequence: the nature of masculinity became problematic. What is it? Is it as unitary and monochromatic as had been assumed, or is it more diverse than had been supposed? How does it develop? When I sought Tony Santangelo's life history, the issue of gender development was not at the center of my interest, but as I studied his life history, cognizant of the growing importance of the masculinity issue, I became aware that he provided some information that merited consideration in this context.

Involvement in competitive sports—as player or fan—became a central feature of American cultural conceptions of masculinity in the second half of the 19th century (Rotundo 1993). Tony Santangelo's life seems to be almost a stereotypical expression of this cultural theme. Among sports, baseball was particularly pervasive in its status as "the national pastime"; it began as a middle-class activity but then spread into the working class (Rotundo 1993, p. 239). Michael Kimmel, in his study of the development of American manhood, writes of the cultural and social importance of baseball:

> Baseball replaced the desiccating immorality of a dissolute life, providing a "remedy for the many evils resulting from the immoral associations boys and young men of our cities are apt to become connected with" and therefore deserving "the endorsement of every clergyman in the country." (Kimmel 1996, p. 140; internal quotation from Adelman 1986)

This passage describing the late 19th and early 20th century United States reads as though it might have been abstracted from Tony Santangelo's life, so closely does it fit his own experience. A substantial portion of his identity from adolescence until middle age was built on his involvement in sports as player, coach and mentor (baseball and hockey) to parish children, and as father of an athletic adolescent boy in whose competitiveness he finds paternal gratification.

Although Tony's sports-based masculinity is almost stereotypical in its nature and is a continuous theme in his adult life, it certainly seems to be discontinuous from his childhood. It was not a straightforward, elaborative development. Tony describes himself as having been a "Mama's boy," which is a way of saying that he wasn't as appropriately masculine as a child as he believes he should have been. He feels he was overprotected, and, in response to my questions about his ethnic identity reports an incident in which he went to his mother to complain about being bullied by an Irish boy. He was not a fighter as a child (or as an adult) and he clearly implies that in that respect he was different from the boys he hung out with. One might wonder how a Mama's boy—slightly built and a nonfighter—becomes a crackerjack baseball player. This is not a natural progression, nor an obvious one. One key may be his self-described role as a mascot to the older boys he hung out with. His experience in this role afforded both security and a chance to participate in their activities, which included some ball playing. Tony reports that he was a better ballplayer than some of the older fellows. So it seems that his participation in this group, which he later left for the St. Ignatius team, gave him an opportunity to develop, display, and become self-confident in his skills. The reputation he thus developed enabled him to transfer from his formative but now disvalued group to the champions-to-be of the neighboring parish.

Tony's self-concept of his early years as a Mama's boy survived in an adult derivative, his self-concept as selfish. Indeed, he makes this connection himself. But in other respects he outgrew that early self-concept. His ability in sports certainly helped him to be a man among men. Also, he gives considerable credit to his army experience in which he learned how to function in a non-indulgent environment. During his army service in Japan, too, baseball became an important expression of his masculine identity.

When we consider Tony's life history as a whole, we can see that in one way or another he dealt with seven main elements in constructing his masculine identity: (1) sports; (2) crime; (3) toughness; (4) work; (5) sexuality; (6) marriage and parenthood; (7) conviviality. He is explicit in saying that he chose involvement in sports over involvement in crime. And while he does not quite say so, he also chose sports over sexuality. He does say that as an adolescent he was too involved in sports to notice girls and that a girl took the initiative in arousing his reluctant interest. Even during his army service in Japan, he chose sports over sexual experimentation and dalliance. As a boy and as a young man, the toughness he saw in others was something that he considered was not part of himself. He wasn't a fighter as a boy and he stayed out of bar brawls as a young man.

Tony never expresses a clear work ambition, but he cites two types of work that he would like to have fallen into, professional baseball and the Santangelo family bar and restaurant. (He does say that he "always wanted to be somebody," and this may be an indirect way of saying that he nurtured an ambition to be a professional baseball player. He speaks of an ownership role in the bar-restaurant only in the context of his uncles' deaths, not as something he had always hoped to achieve in a more routine way through years of working there.) Marriage and parenthood seem important to him as essential to a normal life. He got married and had children because he considered that that is what a man should do in order to lead a decent life. The particulars of family life are very often dissatisfying to him, but being a husband and father is essential to his sense of what he has done right in his life. He experiences his wife as unreasonable in her expectations and his children as resistant to accepting their proper responsibilities. But he admires his wife's good points and his children's accomplishments, and he considers that having a family saved him from a disreputable kind of manhood that would have been his fate as a single man. Finally, conviviality, being part of a group of buddies who hang out together, building goodwill—these are essential to his sense of masculinity, even though they generate friction in his marriage.

Tony's life history narrative, brief as it is, includes a wide array of elements he dealt with in developing his gender identity. We can see the cultural elements that he worked with and some of the major choices he made among them. We can also see that it would be misleading to focus only on his sports involvement and to reach the easy conclusion that Tony is a "typical working-class male." Such a facile conclusion would obscure his path to that involvement, for it is surely a circuitous path from Mama's boy to outstanding ballplayer. The culture at a particular historical time provides the framework and the resources for a man's gender identity, but it does not create the identity. That is created through and out of interactions with significant others and is fashioned through the concomitant inner dialogue of the self.

Identities

Tony Santangelo has experienced many identities in the course of his life—Mama's boy, peer group mascot, celebrity ballplayer in his neighborhood, fellow who considered himself not as smart as others where school is concerned, fellow with street smarts, army draftee, young man who thought the world owed him a living, construction laborer, bartender, husband, father, ironworker, regular at Joe Wagner's, sports mentor to local parish children. The meanings of these various identities have been discussed in various ways in the analysis to this point. With one exception, I do not have more to say about them.

A central issue in understanding the experienced life course is trying to understand how, if at all, identities later in the life course are linked to earlier ones. The linkage of particular interest here concerns Tony's ability to accept the identity of sports teacher or mentor that Father Durney wanted to assign him. What made it possible for Tony to respond to Father Durney's urging to become a sports teacher by perceiving it as an identity he could accept? Why did he not decline it as unsuitable? His earlier identity as a good ballplayer was not sufficient. Many good ballplayers would not necessarily see themselves as possible coaches for the young. In Tony's case, one additional earlier identity seems preparatory, his identity as mascot in a group of older peers. His role-taking in that childhood relationship, in which he claims he learned from the older boys, gave him an experience of being mentored by someone older. That childhood identity, together with his successful ballplayer identity in young adulthood, made it possible for him to respond positively to Father Durney's invitation, despite his never having thought of himself as having anything to teach.

CHOICES AND OUTCOMES

Underlying all the particular issues in understanding the life course are, in my judgment, two general issues: (1) The relationship of childhood to adulthood; (2) The relationship of personal agency to social structure. Although there are some writers (e.g., Alanen 1990; Jenks 1982; Qvortrup 1991, 1995) who argue for thinking about childhood as a social category with its own importance rather than as a preparation for adulthood, and although one can grant considerable merit to this view, it is nonetheless difficult to ignore the widely shared conviction that a life can only be fulfilled in adulthood. The death of a child is more poignant than the death of an old person because the old person had at least the chance of fulfillment while the child did not. Few would say of a dead 12-year-old: "S/he had many friends, was a good athlete and a good student. S/he had a full life." The circumstances, satisfactions, and distresses of childhood have their own intrinsic importance, but there is no escaping the fact that childhood is in some way a preparation for adulthood. How these two great periods of life are connected is one of the great problem areas of the social sciences. Earlier in this part of the study I have proposed some concepts that contribute to understanding that connection and showed how they help to understand the life of Tony Santangelo.

I turn now to the second general issue. Everybody who functions in society has to have at least a very minimal understanding of some aspects of social structure. Knowing and acting in accordance with the different statuses of family and strangers, pupil and teacher, storekeeper and customer are elementary outcomes of socialization. Most people likely acquire some awareness of status hierarchies and social class differences. It is hard to say how many proceed from an operating understanding of social structure to a belief that their life course is significantly shaped by social structure. It is doubtful that many share the belief of sociologists Dennis Hogan and Nan Astone who take a very deterministic position:

> Because we believe that institutional arrangements are of crucial importance in choices people make, throughout this paper we will use *pathway* when we refer to the life course of an individual. We believe that *pathway* (a course laid out for people, strongly encouraging them to take a particular route to get from one place to another) is a more accurate way to describe the particular series of transitions an individual makes than *trajectory* (which implies a greater amount of individual initiative than actually occurs). (Hogan and Astone 1986, p. 110; italics in original)

There are at least two great difficulties with this statement, which is an expression of the expectable life course perspective that was cited in the preface and briefly discussed in Part I. The first problem is that the authors of this literature review give no indication of having tried to find out how much individual initiative "actually occurs," so they are in no position to dismiss it as insignificant. The second problem is that their review of studies pertains to aggregated lives, not to "the life course of an individual." The studies in their purview do not include any that deal with the life course of an individual, and they are therefore in no position to comment on that topic. They have taken studies that deal with aggregations of lives and have tried to use them to foreclose the study of individual lives by simply declaring that these methodologies do so. They seem to be arguing contradictory positions simultaneously: there is no need to study the initiatives that might occur in individual lives, but our institutional concept of pathway describes the life course of an individual.

It is a stretch to apply the concept of pathway to Tony's life course. He believes he made choices, at least some of which might be called initiatives; but even when not meriting that designation, it is questionable whether the term pathway is suitable. To be sure, some information is missing. Who "strongly encouraged" Tony to drop out of high school? Perhaps some teachers did. We don't know. Perhaps the guys he hung out with did. But Tony says it was his choice, a choice he made against his parents' wishes, especially his father's. Even if we assume that he was badly treated by teachers and was thereby led to believe they did not want him in school, and if we further assume that the activities of the peers he hung out with attracted him away from school, how can we call his leaving school a pathway laid out for him when his parents did not want him to drop out? On what grounds would his account of his conflict with his parents about leaving school be considered a less satisfactory account of how he made that life transition than an account that claims he was following a pathway laid out for him?

It is possible to add some complexity. Why were his peers more influential in this decision than his father, whom he loved? We can surmise that his anger at his father for the nighttime arguments with his mother weakened his father's authority in his eyes, leaving him more amenable to peer influence. But that still cannot be construed as a pathway laid out for Tony. It cannot obviate the intrafamilial conflict he experienced in making his decision. Nor does the pathway concept take into account the enduring consequences of his decision—the fact that he now regrets it, lives with his regret, and tries to use his experience as a guide in dealing with his adolescent son. The pathway concept of the life course, like other versions of the expectable life course, does not allow for retracing one's steps. In contrast, the experienced life course allows for the phenomenon of revisiting experiences and giving them new symbolic meaning.

Tony does not believe that his life course was and is entirely in his own hands. He knows that it has been significantly affected by others. He came close to a chance at a major league career and he was turned down. When his uncles who owned the family restaurant died he hoped for a chance at ownership and he was denied. He knows that these two chances for an occupational fulfillment were blocked by the decisions of others. But he also has a sense of himself as someone who made significant choices, some right and some mistaken. He now regards his decision to drop out of high school as a mistake.

Equally fateful, if not more so, he sees his decision to choose a life of sports as a way to avoid a criminal life, which he consciously rejected. Tony sees himself as having made the right choice to accept when Charlie Rooney invited him to play on the St. Ignatius baseball team. And he chose to accept his uncle's invitation to become a waiter and bartender, as well as Father Durney's invitation to teach sports. All of these he regards as right choices, choices which gave him social and emotional fulfillment. His decision to turn down his father's urging to apply for the Department of Sanitation job as well as his decision to quit high school, led, in his understanding and recognition, to financial limitation and frustration.

In sum, Tony made two kinds of decisions. He made some he considers mistakes that led to economic frustration. He made what he considers right decisions that yielded him social and emotional satisfactions. He lives with an awareness of these decisions and their consequences. Although he was clearly influenced by others in all of them, they do not line up as a sequence on a pathway that leads in any obvious or even probable way from point A to point B to point C. They are episodes in his struggle to make a life for himself. A meaningful life for Tony involved more than proceeding through a series of occupational positions. He wanted to live a life that was both moral and convivial, as well as one that would gain him some recognition beyond an immediate circle. These goals had a higher priority for him than financial success, and he made decisions accordingly, decisions which endure as self-knowledge.

SUMMATION

My goal in this study is to contribute to understanding the human life course. When I undertook it, I had several considerations in mind: (1) I had long been occupied with the two puzzles that I discussed in Part I, the issue of continuity and discontinuity in the life course and the issue of how working-class people deal with the hardships in their lives and construct their horizons. (2) I was aware that scholars who defined their domain as study of the life course seldom made use of life histories, while those who gathered and published life histories did not usually have as their focus a concern for theoretical understanding of the life course. The gap between these two bodies of literature seemed to me to be wide and regrettable. (3) Landmark studies of lives were either studies of major world figures, such as Erik Erikson's (1958, 1969) studies of Martin Luther and of Gandhi, or of delinquents and criminals, such as Clifford Shaw's *The Jack-Roller* (1966 [1930]). Anthropologists produced life histories of individuals living in what were, to an American, exotic cultures. Celebrity, notoriety, and foreignness, each in their different ways a form of exoticism, provide an obvious point of departure and an obvious focus for interpretation.

I was challenged by the task of understanding a life that offered none of these obvious "pegs" on which to hang a discussion. What can one say about an ordinary life, a life of a man who lives with no obvious claim on public or scholarly attention? What can one learn from the study of such a life that will be helpful in the study of other lives? The task involves close scrutiny of a particular life and construction of a path from the particular to the general. These two intellectual operations are not neatly sequential: they are interleaved.

The most fundamental point to be made about the study of Tony Santangelo's life history is that it opens a new window on the life course and thereby expands the view that has heretofore been available from the study of aggregate data. The latter provides a structural account, a view of the life course as a sequence of transitions in roles and statuses. Clausen (1986) called this the expectable life course. Other sociological researchers have not used a label. But, whatever the differences among them, they focus on the life course primarily as a social structure.

While a life history locates its recounter in the social structure, it yields not an expectable life course but an experienced life course. It tells us how a person has constructed meaning in his life. Tony Santangelo is unmistakably an American whose location in the social structure can be specified by his statuses as an urban, working-class, Roman Catholic, Italian American resident of the Yorkville section of New York City. We learn of significant status transitions in his life—his dropping out of high school, his succession of jobs, his service in the army, his marriage and parenthood. This kind of information could also be obtained by other methods. What else we learn from the life history could not be. We see Tony's life as he reports it in experience, as he gives meaning to significant others and to events. We see the importance of aleatory encounters such as Tony's with Charlie Rooney, which led him out of his neighborhood peer group into an adjacent parish with an organized sports program. We see how the intervention of the state—drafting him into the army, sending him to the South and then to the occupation of Japan—created a temporary structure in which he gained a sense of development into manhood. We see how his experience as a bartender further contributed to his sense of development. We see the way baseball and other sports constitute a lifelong binding thread in his life. We see the way his adherence to peer group in adulthood works against his marriage, which in life course theory can be understood as a disjunction between marriage as a transition in his life and as a turning point in his life. He still claims for himself the scheduling freedoms of a single man. The change in his self was not commensurate or congruent with the change in his status.

Conceptualizing the life course as a series of transitions carries with it the implication that preceding statuses are left behind. When one finally leaves school for work, school is left behind. When one marries, singlehood is left behind. When one leaves one line of work for another, the former line of work is left behind. When the life course is viewed as a series of transitions, discarded statuses become irrelevant. They are used up by their service as platforms for the next status. But such a view of the life course, useful though it may be, is insufficient. For while statuses may be discarded, the same is not necessarily true of the experiences in them. Statuses may be steppingstones, but experiences are building blocks of the self.

To the concept of the life course as a series of transitions must be added another—the life course as a concatenation of experiences. It is a complex chain, like no other. Some of its links are particular events and some are typifications. Some are missing, some are weak, some are strong. And it can be used in many ways. Tony Santangelo dropped out of high school, and that gives him a permanent educational status and a circumscribed occupational horizon. Yet, although his life history was recounted thirty years after he dropped out of school, that experience has not been discarded. Rather, it is superimposed upon the present. It is incorporated into his parental identity and he uses it to direct and discipline his son. It is incorporated into his occupational identity, as he compares himself with agemates and envies their current ability to retire. At age forty-seven, Tony tells us that he feels scarred by the quarrels his father had with his mother when he was a child. Tony is now a construction worker, no longer a bartender. But he has not let go of his experience as a bartender for that experience gave him an expansive sense of development. Tony creates meaning as he concatenates experience, and thereby he creates his self.

Concatenation is not a very precise concept for thinking about the life course, although I think it or something like it is necessary to capture a fundamental aspect of the life course that is missing from prevailing sociological work in this domain. It is an example of what Blumer calls a sensitizing concept. A sensitizing concept "gives the user a general sense of reference and guidance in approaching empirical instances. Whereas definitive concepts provide prescriptions of what to see, sensitizing concepts merely suggest directions along which to look" (Blumer 1969, p. 148). There is more than one way to use the concept, as I have illustrated in the preceding paragraph. Earlier in Part III, from the study of Tony's life I have proposed a set of concepts that are generic links for any life—sense of origin, sense of upbringing, perspective on childhood, sense of development, experiencing passages of time.

Every man depends on his society for a meaningful life. Every man must make his own life. Every man must remember his life in order to continue living as the person he believes himself to be. I take these to be fundamental principles which shape human lives. I have tried to show how their work-

ings can be seen in life histories by studying the life history that Tony Santangelo recounted to me. Through that study I have sought to produce a
method and the beginnings of theory that others can use and build on.

APPENDIX

Life History Interview Guide

Introductory statement to interviewee: I'm interested in studying how people live their life as they go from one age to another—the kinds of things that have happened over time, and how the person thinks about his own life. There have been many studies done of the lives of famous people, but very little is known about the lives of people who are not prominent, not well known. My goal is to study the lives of people who are not well known. I'm interviewing men who have spent most of their life in Yorkville. I'm asking them to tell me the story of their life, and then I'll be asking some additional questions. This will probably take a few hours, so we won't be doing it all in one sitting. Since it will take some of your time, I would pay you at the rate of $4 an hour for the time we spend interviewing.

1. Tell me the story of your life. Start at the beginning and tell me as much as you remember.
2. Who have been the important people at different times in your life? How were they important?
3. What would you say are the major decisions you have made in your life?
4. What periods of your life do you like to look back on? Why?
5. What periods of your life would you rather not think about? Why?
6. What kind of person would you say you are? How did you come to be that kind of person?
7. How have you changed during the course of your life? What are the most important changes? What caused the changes? How did they come about?
8. In what ways have you remained the same? How would you explain that?
9. Think of times when someone tried to persuade you to do something, and they weren't successful: you didn't want to do what they wanted. Tell me about those times.
10. Now tell me about times when someone did persuade you.
11. I'd like you to look back over your life and think of some of the difficult times you had, some of the problems. How did you get through those times? What ef-

fect do you think all that had on you? Let's start with the earliest one you can remember.

12. What times do you consider the best in your life? What made them turn out that way?

13. In what ways do you think you'll change in the future? In what ways do you think you'll stay the same?

14. What opportunities would you say you have had in your life, opportunities that came your way?

15. What opportunities got away from you? Ones that seemed possible but that didn't pan out?

16. What do you think you have learned from your own life, things that have helped you as you went along?

17. Do you think your life could have been different in some ways? Could you have become a different kind of person? Why or why not?

References

ARTICLES AND BOOKS

Adelman, Melvin. 1986. *A Sporting Time: New York City and the Rise of Modern Athletics, 1820–1870*. Champaign: University of Illinois Press.

Alanen, Leena. 1990. "Rethinking Socialization, The Family and Childhood." Pp. 13–28 in Patricia A. Adler and Peter Adler (eds.), *Sociological Studies of Child Development*, Vol. 3. Greenwich, CT: JAI Press.

Alba, Richard. 1985. *Italian Americans*. Englewood Cliffs, NJ: Prentice-Hall.

Allport, Gordon. 1942. *The Use of Personal Documents in Psychological Science*. New York: Social Science Research Council.

Angell, Robert. 1945. "A Critical Review of the Personal Document Method in Sociology 1920–1940." Pp. 177–232 in Louis Gottschalk, Clyde Kluckhohn, and Robert Angell, *The Use of Personal Documents in History, Anthropology, and Sociology*. New York: Social Science Research Council.

Aries, Philippe. 1962. *Centuries of Childhood*. New York: Random House.

Bartlett, Frederic C. 1932. *Remembering*. Cambridge: Cambridge University Press.

Becker, Howard S. 1966. Introduction to Clifford Shaw, *The Jackroller. A Delinquent Boy's Own Story*. Chicago: University of Chicago Press.

Behar, Ruth. 1990. "Rage and Redemption: Reading the Life Story of a Mexican Marketing Woman." *Feminist Studies* 16, no. 2 (Summer 1990): 223–258.

Behar, Ruth. 1993. *Translated Woman. Crossing the Border with Esperanza's Story*. Boston: Beacon Press.

Bennett, James. 1981. *Oral History and Delinquency*. Chicago: University of Chicago Press.

Berger, Peter, and Luckmann, Thomas. 1967. *The Social Construction of Reality*. Garden City, NY: Doubleday Anchor.

Berteaux, Daniel, and Berteaux-Wiame, Isabelle. 1981. "Life Stories in the Bakers Trade." Pp. 169–189 in Daniel Berteaux (ed.), *Biography and Society. The Life History Approach in the Social Sciences*. Beverly Hills, CA: Sage.

Blumer, Herbert. 1969. *Symbolic Interactionism*. Englewood Cliffs, NJ: Prentice-Hall.

Brim, O. G., Jr., 1974. "Selected Theories of the Male Mid-Life Crisis: A Comparative Analysis." Paper presented at annual Meeting of American Psychological Association, September 1974.

Brim, O. G., Jr. 1976. "Life-Span Development of the Theory of Oneself: Implications for Child Development." Pp. 241–251 in Hayne W. Reese (ed.), *Advances in Child Development and Behavior*, Vol. 11. New York: Academic Press.

Clausen, John. 1974. "Foreword." Glen Elder, Jr. *Children of the Great Depression*. Chicago: University of Chicago Press.

Clausen, John. 1985. *The Life Course: A Sociological Perspective*. Englewood Cliffs, NJ: Prentice-Hall.

Clausen, John. 1995. *American Lives. Looking Back at the Children of the Great Depression*. Berkeley, Los Angeles, London: University of California Press.

Cohler, Bertram. 1982. "Personal Narrative and the Life Course." Pp. 205– 241 in Paul Baltes and O. G. Brim (eds.), *Life-Span Development and Behavior*, Vol. 4. New York: Academic Press.

Cooley, Charles Horton. (1909). *Social Organization*. New York: Scribners.

Crapanzano, Vincent. 1980. *Tuhami. Portrait of a Moroccan*. Chicago: University of Chicago Press.

Crapanzano, Vincent. 1984. "Life Histories." *American Anthropologist* 86: 953–960.

Denzin, Norman. 1989. *Interpretive Biography*. Newbury Park, CA: Sage.

Dollard, John. 1935. *Criteria for the Life History*. New Haven: Yale University Press.

Dubin, Robert. 1956. "Industrial Workers' World: A Study of the Central Life Interests of Industrial Workers." *Social Problems* 3: 131–141.

Dunphy, Dexter. 1972. *The Primary Group*. New York: Appleton-Century-Crofts.

Elder, Glen, Jr. 1974. *Children of the Great Depression*. Chicago: University of Chicago Press.

Elder, Glen, Jr. 1981. "History and the Life Course." Pp. 77–115 in Daniel Berteaux (ed.), *Biography and Society. The Life History Approach in the Social Sciences*. Beverly Hills, CA: Sage.

Elder, Glen, Jr., and O'Rand, Angela M. 1995. "Adult Lives in a Changing Society. Pp. 452–475 in Karen S. Cook, Gary Alan Fine, James S. House (eds.), *Sociological Perspectives on Social Psychology*. Boston: Allyn and Bacon.

Elder, Glen, Jr.; Modell, John; and Parke, Ross D. 1993. *Children in Time and Place*. Cambridge, England, and New York: Cambridge University Press.

Elder, Glen, Jr.; Pavalko, Eliza; and Clipp, Elizabeth C. 1993. *Working with Archival Data. Studying Lives*. Newbury Park, CA: Sage.

Elder, Glen, Jr., and Rockwell, Richard C. 1979. "The Life-Course and Human Development: An Ecological Perspective." *International Journal of Behavioral Development* 2: 1–21.

Erikson, Erik. 1950. *Childhood and Society*. New York: W. W. Norton.

Erikson, Erik. 1958. *Young Man Luther*. New York: W. W. Norton.

Erikson, Erik. 1969. *Ghandi's Truth*. New York: W. W. Norton.

Erikson, Erik. 1980. *Identity and the Life Cycle*. New York: W. W. Norton.

Frenkel, Else. 1936. "Studies in Biographical Psychology." *Character and Personality* 5:1–34.

Freud, Sigmund. 1948 [1915]. "Repression." Pp. 84–97 in S. Freud, *Collected Papers*, Vol. IV. London: The Hogarth Press.

Gans, Herbert. 1962. *The Urban Villagers: Group and Class in the Life of Urban Americans*. New York: Free Press.

Gecas, Viktor. 1982. "The Self-Concept." Pp. 1–33 in Ralph Turner and James F. Short, Jr. (eds.), *Annual Review of Sociology*, Vol. 8. Palo Alto, CA: Annual Reviews, Inc.

Gergen, Kenneth J. 1980. "The Emerging Crisis in Life-Span Developmental Theory," Pp. 31–63 in Paul Baltes and Orville G. Brim, Jr. (eds.) *Life-Span Development and Behavior*, Vol. 3. New York: Academic Press.

Gillis, John. 1974. *Youth and History: Tradition and Change in European Age Relations, 1770–Present*. New York: Academic Press.

Glaser, Barney, and Anselm Strauss. 1971. *Status Passage*. Chicago: Aldine-Atherton.

Gusdorf, Georges. 1980. "Conditions and Limits of Autobiography." Pp. 28–48 in James Olney (ed.), *Autobiography: Essays Theoretical and Critical*. Princeton: Princeton University Press.

Hagestad, Gunhild O., and Neugarten, Bernice. 1985. "Age and the Life Course." Pp. 35–61 in Robert H. Binstock and Ethel Shanas (eds.), *Handbook of Aging and the Social Sciences*, 2nd ed. New York: Van Nostrand.

Handel, Gerald. 1984. "A Children's New York: Boys at Play in Yorkville." Pp. 33–49 in Vernon Boggs, Gerald Handel, and Sylvia F. Fava (eds.), *The Apple Sliced: Sociological Studies of New York City*. New York: Praeger.

Handel, Gerald. 1991. "Abandoned Ambitions: Transition to Adulthood in the Life Course of Working-Class Boys." Pp. 225–245 in Spencer Cahill (ed.), *Sociological Studies of Child Development*, Vol. 4. Greenwich, CT: JAI Press.

Handel, Gerald. 1994. "Life Course as Reflexive Object: Some Constituent Elements in the Life Histories of Working-Class Men." Pp. 295–306 in Norman Denzin (Ed.), *Studies in Symbolic Interaction*, Vol. 16. Greenwich, CT: JAI Press.

Hess, Robert D., and Gerald Handel, 1995. *Family Worlds*. Lanham, MD: University Press of America. (Reissue of 1974 edition published by University of Chicago Press.)

Hogan, Dennis, and Nan Astone. 1986. "The Transition to Adulthood." Pp. 109–130 in *Annual Review of Sociology*, Vol. 12, edited by Ralph H. Turner and James F. Short. Palo Alto, CA: Annual Reviews.

Howell, Joseph T. 1984. *Hard Living on Clay Street*. Prospect Heights, IL: Waveland.

Hughes, Everett. 1958. *Men and Their Work*. Glencoe, IL: The Free Press.

Hughes, Everett. 1962. "What Other?" Pp. 119–127 in Arnold M. Rose (Ed.), *Human Behavior and Social Processes. An Interactionist Approach*. Boston: Houghton Mifflin.

Jenks, Chris. 1982. *The Sociology of Childhood*. London, England: Batsford.

Keniston, Kenneth. 1970. "Youth: A New Stage of Life." *American Scholar* 39 (Autumn 1970): 631–654.

Kessen, William. 1981. "The Child and Other Cultural Inventions." Pp. 26–40 in Frank S. Kessel and Alexander W. Siegel (eds.), *The Child and Other Cultural Inventions*. New York: Praeger.

Kimmel, Michael. 1996. *Manhood in America*. New York: The Free Press.

Kluckhohn, Clyde. 1945. "The Personal Document in Anthropological Science." Pp. 79–173 in Louis Gottschalk, Clyde Kluckhohn, and Robert Angell (eds.), *The Use of Personal Documents in History, Anthropology, and Sociology*. New York: Social Science Research Council.

Kohli, Martin. 1986a. "Social Organization and Subjective Construction of The Life Course." Pp. 271–292 in Aage B. Sørensen, Franz E. Weinert, and Lonnie R. Sherrod (eds.), *Human Development and the Life Course*. Hillsdale, NJ: Lawrence Erlbaum Associates.

Kohli, Martin. 1986b. "The World We Forgot: A Historical Review of the Life Course." Pp. 271–303 in Victor W. Marshall (ed.), *Later Life. The Social Psychology of Aging*. Beverly Hills, CA: Sage.

Langness, L. L. 1965. *The Life History in Anthropological Science*. New York: Holt, Rinehart, and Winston.

Langness, L. L., and Frank, Gelya. 1981. *Lives. An Anthropological Approach*. Novato, CA: Chandler & Sharp Publishers, Inc.

Levinson, Daniel J., with Charlotte N. Darrow, Edward B. Klein, Maria H. Levinson, Braxton McKee. 1978. *The Seasons of a Man's Life*. New York: Ballantine.

Lewis, Oscar. 1961. *The Children of Sanchez. Autobiography of a Mexican Family*. New York: Random House.

Mayer, Karl Ulrich, and Müller, Walter. 1986. "The State and the Structure of the Life Course." Pp. 217–245 in Aage B. Sørensen, Franz E. Weinert, and Lonnie R. Sherrod (eds.), *Human Development and the Life Course*. Hillsdale, NJ: Lawrence, Erlbaum Associates.

Maynes, Mary. 1989. "Gender and Narrative Form in French and German Working-Class Autobiographies." Pp. 103–117 in Personal Narratives Group, *Interpreting Women's Lives*. Bloomington: Indiana University Press.

McAdams, Dan P. 1988. *Power, Intimacy, and the Life Story*. New York: Guilford Press.

Mead, George Herbert. 1934. *Mind, Self, and Society*. Chicago: University of Chicago Press.

Meyer, John W. 1986. "The Self and the Life Course: Institutionalization and Its Effects." P. 203 in Aage B. Sørensen, Franz E. Weinert and Lonnie R. Sherrod (eds.), *Human Development and the Life Course*. Hillsdale, NJ: Lawrence Erlbaum Associates.

Miller, S. M. 1964a. "The 'New' Working Class," Pp. 2–9 in Arthur Shostak and William Gomberg (eds.), *Blue-Collar World*. Englewood Cliffs, NJ: Prentice-Hall.

Miller, S. M. 1964b. "The American Working Classes: A Typological Approach." Pp. 9–23 in Arthur Shostak and William Gomberg (eds.), *Blue-Collar World*. Englewood Cliffs, NJ: Prentice-Hall.

Miller, S. M. and Riessman, Frank. 1968. *Social Class and Social Policy*. Chap. 6, School Dropouts and American Society. New York: Basic Books.

Musgrove, Frank. 1964. *Youth and Social Order*. Bloomington: Indiana University Press.

Nasaw, David. 1994. *Going Out*. Cambridge: Harvard University Press.

Patai, Daphne. 1988a. "Constructing a Self: A Brazilian Life Story." *Feminist Studies* 14, No. 1 (Spring 1988) Pp. 143–166.

Patai, Daphne. 1988b. *Brazilian Women Speak. Contemporary Life Stories*. New Brunswick, NJ, and London: Rutgers University Press.

Perinbanayagam, Robert. 1975. "The Significance of Others in the Thought of Alfred Schutz, G. H. Mead and C. H. Cooley. *The Sociological Quarterly* 16 (Autumn 1975): 500–521.

Personal Narratives Group. 1989. *Interpreting Women's Lives*. Bloomington: Indiana University Press.

Plath, David. 1980. *Long Engagements. Maturity in Modern Japan*. Stanford: Stanford University Press.

Plummer, Ken. 1983. *Documents of Life*. London: George Allen & Unwin.

Plummer, Ken. 1990. "Herbert Blumer and the Life History Tradition." *Symbolic Interaction* 13 (2): 125–144.

Qvortrup, Jens. 1991. *Childhood as a Social Phenomenon—An Introduction to a Series of National Reports*. Second Edition. Vienna, Austria: European Centre for Social Welfare Policy and Research.

Qvortrup, Jens. 1995. "Childhood in Europe: A New Field of Social Research." Pp. 9–21 in Lynne Chisolm, Peter Buchner, Heinz-Hermann Kruger, and Manuela du Bois-Reymond (eds.), *Growing Up in Europe*. Berlin and New York: Walter de Gruyter.

Rieff, Philip. 1961. *Freud: The Mind of the Moralist*. Garden City, NY: Doubleday Anchor.

Rosenberg, Morris. 1973. "Which Significant Others?" *American Behavioral Scientist* 16 (6): 829–860.

Rosenberg, Morris. 1979. *Conceiving the Self*. New York: Basic Books.

Ross, Bruce M. 1991. *Remembering the Personal Past*. New York: Oxford University Press.

Rotundo, E. Anthony. 1993. *American Manhood*. New York: Basic Books.

Rubin, Lillian. 1976. *Worlds of Pain*. New York: Basic Books.

Schachtel, Ernest G. 1959. "On Memory and Childhood Amnesia." Pp. 279–332 in E. G. Schachtel, *Metamorphosis*. New York: Basic Books.

Schacter, Daniel. 1996. *Searching for Memory. The Brain, the Mind, and the Past*. New York: Basic Books.

Sennett, Richard, and Cobb, Jonathan. 1973. *The Hidden Injuries of Class*. New York: Vintage.

Shaw, Clifford. 1966 [1930]. *The Jack-Roller. A Delinquent Boy's Own Story*. Chicago: University of Chicago Press.

Shils, Edward A. 1951. "The Study of the Primary Group." Pp. 44–59 in Daniel Lerner and Harold D. Lasswell (eds.), *The Policy Sciences*. Stanford, CA: Stanford University Press.

Sørensen, Aage B. 1986. "Social Structure and Mechanisms of Life-Course Processes." Pp. 177–197 in Aage B. Sørensen, Franz E. Weinert, Lonnie B. Sherrod (eds.), *Human Development and the Life Course*. Hillsdale, NJ: Lawrence E. Erlbaum.

Starr, Jerold M. 1983. "Toward a Social Phenomenology of Aging: Studying the Self Processes in Biographical Work." *International Journal of Aging and Human Development* 16 (4): 255–270.

Statistical Abstract of the United States, 1994. National Data Book. 1994. Washington: U.S. Government Printing Office.

Strauss, Anselm. 1959. *Mirrors and Masks*. Glencoe, IL: The Free Press.

Thomas, William I., and Znaniecki, Florian. 1918–1920. *The Polish Peasant in Europe and America*, 5 volumes. Boston: Richard G. Badger.

Traugott, Mark. 1993. *The French Worker: Autobiographies from an Early Industrial Era*. Berkeley and Los Angeles: University of California Press.

Tucker, Susan. 1988. *Telling Memories Among Southern Women: Domestic Workers and Their Employers in the Segregated South*. New York: Schocken Books.

Watson, Lawrence C., and Watson-Franke, Maria-Barbara. 1985. *Interpreting Life Histories. An Anthropological Inquiry*. New Brunswick, NJ: Rutgers University Press.

Wetzler, Scott E., and Sweeney, John A. 1988. "Childhood Amnesia: An Empirical Demonstration. Pp. 191–201 in David C. Rubin (ed.), *Autobiographical Memory*. Cambridge, England, and New York: Cambridge University Press.

White , Robert W. 1952. *Lives in Progress: A Study in the Natural Growth in Personality*. New York: Holt.

NEWSPAPERS

"Change Comes as a Loss to Yorkville Old-Timers," *New York Times*, Sunday, Dec. 21, 1980.

"Durable Landmark to Irish Glory Fading Out on the East Side," *New York Times*, Tuesday, Feb. 12, 1991. Section B, p. 3.

Johnson, Kirk. (1985). "If you're thinking of living in: Upper Yorkville." *New York Times*, Sunday, Dec. 1. Real Estate Section.

Kennedy, Shawn G. (1984). "The Fall of a Yorkville Landmark: Ethnic Makes Way for Modern," *New York Times*, Sunday, Sept. 16, Section 8.

Kennedy, Shawn G. (1990). "A New Cachet for Old East 86th Street," *New York Times*, Sunday, April 15, Section 10.

Rimer, Sara. (1983). "Yorkville Turns Chic and Costly," *New York Times*, Sunday, November 6, 1983. Section 8.

Index

About the Author

GERALD HANDEL is Professor of Sociology at The City College and The Graduate Center of the City University of New York. Among his many published books, he was coeditor of *The Apple Sliced: Sociological Studies of New York City* (Praeger, 1983). He has also published many articles and book reviews.